Also by Mary Behan

A Measured Thread

& companion book: *Finding Isobel*

Kernels

ABBEY GIRLS

An Irish Boarding School Memoir

Mary Behan
Valerie Behan

Laurence Gate Press

Behan, Mary

Abbey girls : an Irish boarding school memoir / Mary Behan, Valerie Behan.

pages : illustrations, map ; cm

Includes bibliographical references.

ISBN: 978-1-7344943-9-6 (paperback),
978-1-3106603-6-8 (ebook),
also available as an audio book

1. Behan, Mary. 2. Behan, Valerie. 3. Students--Ireland--Biography. 4. Catholic schools--Ireland--History--20th century. 5. Boarding schools--Ireland--History--20th century. 6. Correspondence. 7. Autobiography. I. Behan, Valerie. II. Title.

LC506.I73 B44 2015

371.071209417

Copyright © 2015 Mary Behan & Valerie Behan

All rights reserved.

No part of this book may be reproduced in any form or by any means without permission from the publisher. Contact the publisher at mvbehan.com

Interior design by Christine Keleny
of CKBooks Publishing

Laurence Gate Press
6383 Hillsandwood Rd.
Mazomanie, WI 53560

For our parents,

Mick and Carmel

§

All our love

Contents

Part One: Before

    Drogheda, Ireland 1959   3
    Our Parents   7
    St. Philomena's Primary School   20
    Loreto Abbey Rathfarnham   26

Part Two: The Abbey

    Arrival   30
    The Refectory   36
    Chapel   45
    Dormitory Life   52
    Nuns   61
    Teachers   77
    Merit, Order and Deportment   89
    Confession   96
    Retreats   106
    Rituals and Traditions   112
    Games   120
    The Parlour   131
    Music   138
    The Gym   148
    Clothes   157
    The Infirmary   162
    Holidays   166
    What is Memory?   172

Map of Ireland

Preface

Half a century ago two little girls entered a convent in Ireland, not to become nuns but to be educated by them. The next six years at Loreto Abbey Rathfarnham were formative. Maybe the Jesuit maxim 'Give me a child for the first seven years and I will give you the man' is still apt.

In conversations about our past we realize how different our memories are. Yet, we are close, just two years apart in age. We had the same upbringing in Drogheda, a provincial town in Ireland, during the 1950s. We both spent six years from ages 11 to 17 at Loreto Abbey Rathfarnham, a girls boarding school in Dublin that was distinguished by its commitment to education. Following boarding school we both went on to University College Dublin and careers in science. With her Ph.D. in Soil Zoology from McGill University, Montreal, Valerie spent 30 years as a Research Scientist with Agriculture

Canada, Ottawa. Mary completed her Ph.D. in Zoology at University College Dublin, and spent her career as a Professor of Neuroscience at the University of Wisconsin, Madison.

Friends consider us very similar. We think of ourselves as similar; we are curious, opinionated, knowledgeable and in different ways, without fear. We owe who we are primarily to our extraordinary parents, who gave us the freedom to walk off the edge of the known universe. We also owe the teachers and students we met at Loreto Abbey Rathfarnham not just for an excellent education but for many other qualities that have served us well: discipline, efficiency, collegiality, responsibility, competitiveness.

Now retired, we remain close friends. A few years ago we began a correspondence about our boarding school years that forms the core of this book. It was a complete surprise to both of us that we remember events so differently. We shared the same experiences and rituals, but our memories of these are sometimes polar opposites. As Mary asks in her final letter: "What is Memory?". The intervening years have exposed us to many different events, and quite literally altered the neural connections in our brains. Yet, by writing these letters to each other we have opened "magic casements" into our past that allowed us to immerse ourselves in this fascinating cloistered world once again.

Part One: Before

Drogheda, Ireland 1959

We grew up in Ireland during the 1950s, a time when the country was a poor, quiet, under-developed backwater at the edge of Europe. Its youth were educated by a Catholic hierarchy of nuns and priests. There were few jobs, and emigration to the USA, Canada, Australia and Great Britain was a factor in every family. The population was about 2.9 million, significantly reduced from the 8 million or so before the Great Famine, over a century prior. These were the years after World War II when everything was scarce. Ireland had been neutral during the war, to our father's chagrin. Although about 50,000 Irish joined the British forces, our grandmother would not endorse Dad joining up. "Dev" (Eamonn De Valera), was our Taoiseach or Prime Minister during that period, and he despised the British whom he had fought during the years following the Easter Rising in 1916. Although England was the country's main trading partner, Ireland withdrew from the Commonwealth in 1948. This, no doubt, resulted in much of the isolation Ireland experienced in our childhood years, before it joined the European Union in 1973. Perhaps because of Ireland's WWII neutrality, there was intense censorship and xenophobia in the country. At the same time, people lived with a certain duality. For example, there was a Prisoner of War camp at Gormenstown, about fifteen miles from our home town of Drogheda. Our grandmother invited officers to a meal at weekends, with German and English POWs visiting the house on alternate Sundays. Ireland may have been neutral but it was in England's shadow and so all imports were limited during the 1950s. We crossed the border into Northern Ireland for special treats such as Mars Bars and tinned fruit.

As children, the center of our universe was Drogheda, County Louth. The town and its surroundings were our playground. Drogheda was like many medium sized towns in Ireland, with a population of about 15,000, numerous pubs and seven churches. But unlike many other Irish towns, Drogheda was steeped in history. The Boyne River was the reason for the town's existence. The river is tidal to just upstream of the town, and could be forded there since time immemorial. The Anglo-Normans established a bridge and gave the town its name, Droichead Átha, the Bridge of the Ford. During the fifteenth century Drogheda, together with Dublin, Waterford and Kilkenny were considered the most important towns in Ireland. Drogheda was a walled town since at least the end of the twelfth century and parts of the walls and city gates still remain. The town was important enough to be captured by Cromwell in 1649, who then massacred everyone within the walls. The Battle of the Boyne that brought the reign of the Catholic James II to an end, establishing the Protestant William of Orange as the King of England, was fought just three miles west of the town in 1690. East of the town were the sandy beaches of Termonfeckin, Mornington, Bettystown and Baltray. West of the town were the ancient Neolithic burial grounds of Newgrange and Knowth, sites that are older than the pyramids; all were our playground.

Christianity played a big part in the Boyne Valley since the time of St. Patrick, and the area is dotted with churches and monasteries. Monasterboice graveyard with its striking Celtic cross, and the tenth century remains of Mellifont Abbey were just a couple of miles north of Drogheda. St. Peter's parish church where we went to Mass every Sunday, has a blackened, shriveled head in a side altar; Blessed Oliver Plunkett had been martyred while resisting Cromwell. On the other side of the river was St. Mary's parish church, and scattered around the town were churches for the various Catholic religious orders, the Augustinians, Franciscans and Dominicans. There was a single Protestant church in the town, also called St. Peter's, but in our eyes it couldn't rival our St. Peter's as it had no gory relics.

Being almost forgotten and irrelevant at the extremity of Europe, Ireland during the 1950s was wonderfully safe. There was a stable government, the Troubles had not yet started up again in Northern Ireland. Fintan O'Toole in his masterful "Irish Times Book of the Century" described Ireland of the 1950s as having the "prevailing atmosphere of church-inspired repression," but we were too young to notice. We were also too young to be affected by the politics of Partition, the intense censorship of books and theatre, and the lack of birth control, abortion and divorce. We wanted for nothing because we didn't know what there was to want. Although television arrived in Drogheda in 1956 and we had one of the first sets, it was commercial-free. Radio was limited to Radio Éireann, and it wasn't until Dad organized home-built radios for us with better signals, that we realized that commercial radio stations like Radio Luxembourg existed.

Our Parents

Our parents' families were Irish and Catholic. Michael, our father, was born in Granard, County Mayo, and his mother was "one of the O'Connors of Swinford." This affiliation, spoken with gravitas so many times by O'Connor relatives, made us question the Behan side of the relationship throughout our lives, and we are no closer to resolving that enigma. The O'Connors viewed themselves as Irish nobility; they were literate for generations, and our grandparents' generation were mainly solicitors and priests. They had cared for the money of Swinford Catholics when English-owned banks wouldn't deal with them. Our Behan grandfather, from County Kildare as far as we know, was a gentle man, and spent much of his life as a bank manager at the Bank of Ireland in Drogheda.

Our Behan grandparents lived an "upstairs

downstairs" existence in one of the grander houses on Laurence Street in Drogheda. They had two servants who lived and worked downstairs, and who responded to bells. Unknown to our grandparents, they also had a dog who attacked our grandfather on one of his rare visits downstairs. When our dad was a teenager, the whole family moved to a big house on the outskirts of town called Greenhills. Like many of his contemporaries, Dad went to the Christian Brothers day school in Drogheda followed by four years at Castleknock boarding school for boys in Dublin.

Carmel, our mother, was one of the Bourkes of Castlebar, County Mayo. Her dad broke away from the rest of the family and started a bicycle repair business, which was considered beneath the Bourkes at the time, and resulted in him being ostracized by many in the family. But when cars came to Ireland, he became the Ford dealer for the west of Ireland, and subsequently became well-off. Mummy was educated in a day school in Castlebar, and spent her last two years at Kylemore Abbey boarding school on the shores of Lough Cong in County Mayo. She was the youngest student in Dentistry when she went to University College Dublin at age 16, and it was at the Dental Hospital that she met Dad, who was a dental student at the Royal College of Surgeons in Dublin. The Bourkes lived in as grand a house as the Behan/O'Connor clan. Nonetheless, as business was considered more lower class than the professions, our O'Connor grandmother had to die before Dad could marry his university sweetheart.

Ireland of the 1950s was as class ridden as any

episode of Downton Abbey. Mummy moved to Drogheda when she got married, and would always be a "runner" in the eyes of those born in the town. Both our parents were practicing dentists before they got married, but dentistry was a non-essential need in Ireland at that time. People were very poor; most only came to the dentist to get a set of dentures (known as false teeth), and the town could not support both our parents in practice. Dentists were often paid in kind rather than in cash, and so there was a continuous supply of horrendous Christmas cakes with rock-hard white icing in the house, but also butter, eggs and the occasional chicken, or salmon poached from the Boyne River no doubt. Of course, dentistry improved when the National Health scheme came into force. Dad was also affiliated with the Lourdes Hospital in Drogheda, the largest teaching hospital in the Province of Leinster, where he did more complicated dental procedures that required general anesthesia. The Lourdes was the Mother House of the Medical Missionaries of Mary, a religious nursing order, with branches mainly in Africa. As a result, we had a steady stream of young African residents coming to our house for Sunday dinner and conversation.

We lived with our Behan grandfather in the big house at Greenhills until the oldest of us, Val, turned four. It was the kind of house Mummy was used to, with an enormous kitchen surrounded by sculleries and pantries for preparing and storing food. Grandad had two enormous greenhouses, an orchard and extensive flower gardens. Mummy had a series of maids: girls from country villages recommended to our parents by the parish priest, who "showed promise." Being in service in the Behan household would have taught them how a middle-class house was run, how to prepare exotic food (e.g., to wash lettuce and eat it raw rather than boiling it forever like cabbage), and it guaranteed them a recommendation for more lucrative work, such as service in a hotel. They lived with us, and their gentlemen callers, if any, would have been carefully scrutinized by Mummy.

In 1952 when Grandad died, and we were four and two years old, our world changed. Dad did not have the money to buy his sister's and brothers' share of the Greenhills property, so the house with its numerous out-buildings, stables, gardens and fields was sold. Our new house was just up the hill on an acre of land that had been carved off from the extensive fields where the new owners now fattened cattle before their shipment to England. The new house was called Green Gables after a favorite book of our mother's, "Anne of Green Gables" by Lucy Maud Montgomery; this was where we really grew up in the 1950s.

Green Gables was one of a cluster of three houses built with a government-backed mortgage. To qualify, houses could not be larger than 1,200 square feet, tiny by our parents' standards. But Dad was able to add a garage and a separate dental mechanic's annex. The back of the house was lined with a series of improvised sheds housing Dad's collectibles, which had been carefully moved from the old house in Greenhills: boxes of discarded syringes, pillars of discarded oil cans, shelves of airplane parts rescued from planes that had come down over Ireland during

WWII, and the guts of every possible engine available to a born mechanic. Mummy avoided this part of the property, but to Dad it was Mecca. Come the revolution or a world meltdown, he was prepared.

It was a brilliant place to grow-up. We were in the country, a mile from the center of town, and the surrounding roads and woods were safe. The enclave of family houses for the managers of the local cement factory was close by. Our nearest neighbors were the new owners of Greenhills, the O'Kanes, and as the younger girls were our age, we continued to treat the outbuildings there as our own. We didn't need a doll's house, or a make-believe place for serving tea; we had the "four room clover," a two-story building that had housed servants and horse-tackle, all to ourselves. We shuttled back and forth between O'Kane's house and ours — our mother was more exciting, but their mother taught us how to play poker. We played children's lawn games on our small lawn, and went to their larger lawns for tennis and croquet. They always had cake for tea, and when one of us pointed this out to our mother (for we, as the children of dentists, rarely had cake), the response was "well, if it's that good, go live there!"

Like most houses in Ireland at that time, we had no fridge. Food was bought daily, and items like butter and fresh milk were kept under a mesh screen in the scullery. We got unpasteurized milk and free-range eggs from a local farmer, and twice a week the Lyons Bakery van came up our road selling bread, cakes and jams. They had started with two horses pulling a closed cart, but by the time we moved from the big house, Lyons was motorized. Life revolved around the kitchen. There was a long, folding table by the front window where the four of us ate. Dad and Mummy sat at either end reading the newspaper and passing comments to each other while we sat between them, reading comics in silence, as comments from us were not appreciated by Mummy.

In Ireland during the 1950s, rural dentists who did their own technical work such as making crowns (usually of gold or silver), and crafting dentures and bridges were unusual. As business improved, Dad, who did his own technical work, trained John Mc Ginn as his dental technician. Our caché rose considerably amongst our friends as none of them had a "John Mc Ginn" in their life. On wet days during school holidays we were allowed into John's workshop to play. We would sit at a small bench with all the essential ingredients for making and painting plaster molds of Walt Disney characters, farmyard animals, and figurines in the nativity. John took the mess we made in his stride: spilled plaster of Paris and paint, water everywhere, questionable forms hardening in his work space, while he worked methodically to create bridges, dentures and crowns.

The plaster of Paris forms from all those dental prostheses did not go to waste. Dad spread them around the base of the 25 or so apple trees in the back half acre. Over time, each tree was protected by a foot high wall of chalky white, toothy mandibles and maxillae. Dad hated to throw out anything and his logic was that plaster of Paris, being essentially calcium, would leach into the soil and fertilize the trees. However, the presence of a cement factory less than a mile away suggested that limestone was not deficient in the soils of County Louth, and certainly these forms never seemed to shrink. The best that could be said was that they were a unique deterrent to night time orchard raids by the local schoolboys!

Until 1955 we always went to our grandparents' home called Killadangan, outside Westport, County Mayo, for holidays. Occasionally we would stop into Swinford for lunch with O'Connor relatives, especially the sisters Moya and Cara. They lived in a rambling old bungalow on the edge of town called The Cottage (as their parents and grandparents had), and our visits were an opportunity to recollect their childhoods and O'Connor family affairs. They were unaccustomed to young children, so we were always on our best behavior, careful to sit politely, hoping that they might produce cake. Killadangan, in contrast, was a joyous place, a grand three-story house overlooking Clew Bay on the Atlantic Ocean, which we called "Granny's Sea." As a backdrop there was Croagh Patrick, the site of the annual Reek pilgrimage, and known to us as "Granny's Mountain." St. Patrick was meant to have spent 40 days and nights on Croagh Patrick and to have banished snakes from Ireland on his return to civilization. Lucky for his religious convictions, there have been no snakes in Ireland since it separated from the continental landmass after the last glaciation about 6000 years ago.

Granny Bourke had a cook and several maids, so this was a complete holiday for our parents. For us children it was heaven: we had unlimited space outside, with freedom to ramble and explore. At Christmas all the Bourke relatives came to party, and as Mummy was the second youngest of six children, most of whom had big families, we had a platoon of cousins to play with.

Today the journey from Drogheda to Westport takes about two hours, but then it was more of a five-hour slog along country roads, and through the small rural towns of Ireland. The route is unforgettable though, and even now every turn of the road elicits warm memories: Drogheda, Slane, Kells, Castlepollard, Edgeworthstown, Longford, sometimes by Granard, Strokestown, Ballymoe, Ballyhaunis, Claremorris, Kiltimagh, Castlebar, Westport, and finally Killadangan. Mummy's smile grew as we went west, and her accent deepened. By Kiltimagh we were truly in the stone walled countryside of her home, County Mayo. Her love of that spartan Mayo landscape was intense, rivaled only by her scorn for the soft, undulating landscape of eastern Ireland. You knew you were in the west long before Kiltimagh by the smell of turf fires. The west of Ireland is blanket bog country, and we would pass farmers cutting the peat into slabs and stacking them to dry before loading them into creels hauled by patient donkeys.

Our dad, Mick, as he was known to everyone, loved life. He was a brilliant all-rounder, tall and strong with a grand smile and a firm handshake; everyone wanted him as their friend. He was the second eldest of the O'Connor/Behan family, and as the oldest boy always felt a responsibility for his siblings, and their children in turn. His mother ordained that he would continue in the family tradition and be a bank manager. His brother Johnny was engineering material, and Billy was going to be the dentist. However, Dad and Uncle Billy organized a swap; Uncle Billy was not all that good with his hands, and Dad felt sure that he would enjoy the technical part of dentistry. Dad was the tinkerer in the family and anything mechanical fascinated him. He was unlike anyone else's father in Drogheda; life around him was always exciting, and we never knew what would explode, or what would work perfectly. We had our own stories about him because we had played a part in them. But we also knew that almost every family, poor or rich, on our side of the river Boyne, had other stories about him too. Both he and Mummy taught us to share: Mummy in the practical sense of sharing sweets on a bus with other children who didn't have any, Dad in the emotional sense, because we had to share him.

We are baby-boomers. Mummy was a baby-boomer born too early. Her idea of pleasure was any of the following: a good book, intelligent company and conversation, or theatre or museums. Pleasure did not involve children. She said on more than one occasion that, though she loved us, she would have preferred no children, muttering something about "if the bloody rhythm method had worked…!" As adolescents, we were just in time for female contraception; she had to rely on the archaic rhythm method, known for its unreliability. She wanted us to be grown-up as soon as possible so that she could carry on an adult conversation with us. Her realism and lack of prevarication, while sometimes challenging, made her a wonderful mother. She taught us reading from "The Wind in the Willows" rather than "Cat in the Hat" because she found the former more interesting. She was brutally honest in answering questions such as "Am I pretty?" or "Do I look good in this?" However, she managed to give us that ineffable attribute, good taste, and to be aware of color and beauty. She was immensely proud of both of us and of our careers, and though she is dead many years, we still behave as though we will meet her unexpectedly, and see that look of approval or disapproval on her face. She had wanted to study English and History at University College Dublin, but her father decided that she would be a dentist. She was a thwarted Literature major all her life, and as a result was brilliant when helping us with English homework!

There was no shortage of boys in our life because of Dad. Wednesday and Saturday were half-days in Drogheda when all the businesses closed. You could see the look of freedom on Dad's face on Wednesdays; it was his afternoon to go with Mummy to Dublin. The first stop was the library of The Royal Dublin Society in Ballsbridge, to return and borrow books. Then he would slip off to a scrap dealer, while Mummy went shopping with us. Any scrap that he had purchased would appear sometime during the following week in a clandestine delivery. Some of these deliveries were memorable. During WWII a number of military planes had come down in Ireland as well as some stray bombs. Bits of these would end up in our garage. Dad's scrap merchant dealt in job lots, so Dad often got multiples of an item, or even things he hadn't planned to purchase. So there were lots of "toys" to share with boys in the neighborhood who had any mechanical interest. They would bike to our house and depart with a box or a bomb casing filled with miscellaneous gadgets, strapped to the back of their bicycle. The boys ignored us, but all were on first name terms with our dad — Mick.

These deliveries could be so spectacular that Mummy would warn Dad "I'm leaving you," and start walking down the driveway to the gate. One year, Dad decided that he would make elderflower wine; he had received a few bottles from a patient in lieu of payment, and decided he could do this himself. He needed containers, so the delivery truck arrived with about 100 large wine casks and, thrown in for free, 500 World War I periscopes. Half the households in Drogheda got a periscope to add to their previous "treasures," and we used them for spying over our neighbors' walls. WWII cast-offs were the reason we had the best playground of all our friends and relatives. We had a large sandpit of course, but with bits from downed planes Dad made us a see-saw, a roundabout, and best of all, a swing where the seat came from a flight cockpit. We also had the ultimate boasting point, the cockpit and fuselage of a downed glider, which Dad had rescued from a field in County Wicklow where it had been abandoned after the trainee pilot crash-landed.

If Dad left us and Mummy at Killadangan for a couple of weeks, returning to Drogheda to work, Mummy was always apprehensive as to what changes would have been made to our small house in her absence? One year we returned from the west to find a second-hand Rayburn stove in the kitchen. These stoves were popular because you could burn literally anything in them (telephone directories were one of Dad's favorite fuel sources!). We were all thrilled with the idea of warmth. But in order to install a chimney, Dad opened up access to the attic from the kitchen. In doing so, he created the best place in the house for us and our friends and cousins to play. The roof had a low pitch and adults could only stand up in the middle, so Mummy generally avoided the attic. But at our height we really had the full run of the place. It was our playroom, decorated with his brother Billy's collection of golf trophies (Billy was living in India at the time), and old issues of National Geographic and Time magazine. This was where the television resided, and we watched it while sitting on an old upholstered train seat, another scrap purchase.

We were one of earliest households in Drogheda to get a television. Reception was poor and the programs available from the BBC, Ulster Television and Radio Teilifís Éireann were abysmal. We remember "Captain Pugwash" and "Blue Peter," "Emergency Ward Ten," "The Lone Ranger" and "Hopalong Cassidy." Luckily, the BBC soon put on "Panorama," "Whicker's World," "the Brains Trust" and "Quatermass"; otherwise Mummy would have thrown the television out. Dad devised an ingenious control system. The power switch for the television was routed down to the kitchen, just beside where Mummy would be preparing our tea. From there she could see which program was on by means of a periscope that extended from the kitchen to the attic; Dad had modeled this on the WWI periscopes we had in abundance. It worked brilliantly — Mummy could control our television viewing without having to deal with our noisy chatter, or the sounds of bullets and explosions from the various programs we watched.

The winemaking endeavors were less successful. No one enjoyed the tedium of picking elderflowers, so Dad moved on to blackberry wine. We got pocket money for picking berries, and took turns stomping on these in vast stainless steel vats — another scrap merchant deal. But whether any product was of drinking quality is questionable. Bad wine was distilled in a rudimentary still that Dad constructed in the dental workshop. The product, flavored and colored (Crème De Menthe seems to have been a favorite) would be offered to guests who, in response to subtle hand waving from our mother in the background, politely declined. The really bad stuff was used as weed killer. Winemaking endeavors were banned permanently by Mummy the day the blackberry wine bottles exploded in the attic and purple liquid flowed through the ceiling tiles into the kitchen.

ST. PHILOMENA'S PRIMARY SCHOOL

There were two girls' primary schools in Drogheda: St. Mary's and St. Philomena's; co-ed was not an option in the Ireland of the 1950s. The former had a better academic reputation, so Mummy would have preferred that we attend it. But the Parish priest for St. Philomena's put pressure on Dad: "the school needs support from the middle-class" and "the children of many of your patients will be there," and so on. As a result, we went to a school with low approval rating from the homework guru — Mummy. We started primary school a little after our fourth birthdays by which time, thanks to Mummy, we were already reading English and had the rudiments of Arithmetic. She need not have worried too much. In St. Philomena's we learned to write well, first with chalk on a small, lined slate, graduating to pen and ink from inkwells in each desk. We also learned to read and write in Irish (Gaelic). Maths consisted of endless recitation of multiplication tables, and mental arithmetic that comprised totting up columns of pounds, shillings and pence. One of us learned to sew, presenting totally useless frilly aprons to Mummy on a regular basis. The other was left-handed, a condition considered a bit satanic by the nuns, and as a result spent gruelling sewing classes with her left hand bound, in a failed attempt to persuade her to sew with her right hand. We also had catechism, prayers, drawing, and knitting to the mantra of "in the little hole, around the big tree, up comes bunny, and off goes he." Mummy couldn't have given a fig about anything except English and Maths, and they were the only part of report cards she read carefully. Our primary school certificate shows that we had written exams in Irish, English and Mathematics, and that History, Geography, Music and Needlework were also obligatory for girls. St. Philomena's got around the music requirement through Irish dance, and we have many speech and drama certificates from the Guildhall School of Music and Drama in London.

Auntie Frank Matthews taught us dancing. She wasn't really our aunt, just aunt to our cousins, but we delighted in being related to her in some way. She was single, petite, had studied ballet, and fearlessly introduced us to the joy of pliées, foxtrot, waltz, polka, Charleston and swing, together with Irish jigs, reels and hornpipes. She had no props other than an old gramophone, and a stack of books to put on our heads as she encouraged us to walk around with grace and poise. We all loved her, as she turned even the heftiest of us into swans, at least in our own minds.

For a couple of years we had French lessons once a week from Countess Tolstoy. She and her husband were Russian aristocrats whose family had fled during the Russian revolution. They had somehow ended up in Collon, a village close to Drogheda. The Tolstoys were effectively penniless, and made a living selling organic chickens and produce that they grew themselves. Dad was their dentist, and suggested that in lieu of payment, Countess Tolstoy could teach us French. There were about twelve children in the class, mainly the children of doctors, dentists and solicitors, of whom the Tolstoys were either patients or clients. Class was held on Saturday morning while the Count was selling his wares at the local market, and for a brief hour and a half we copied Countess Tolstoy's wonderful French accent and grammatical clarity.

We lived about two miles from St. Philomena's school. There were no school buses in Ireland at the time so Dad would drop us off in the morning on his way to work. For the first year or so we went to school just for the morning, after which Mummy would walk in to town and bring us home on the bus for our midday dinner. By the time we were eight we could take the bus to and from school by ourselves. There were no school meals; most children were like us and had a relative living in the town where they ate their midday dinner, the main meal of the day in most Irish homes at that time.

The quality of education available at secondary schools in Drogheda ensured that we were going to be sent to boarding school. The local secondary school was just down the road from our house in Greenhills, and had a beautiful location along the Boyne River with wonderful playing fields. But, there were no stellar past pupils, no steady record of graduates going to university, and none of the professionals in Drogheda was an alumnus. Even more compelling, a few pupils had become pregnant while attending school there. Granted, there was neither contraception nor abortion available in Ireland at the time, so teenage pregnancy was an issue not just in our town, but throughout the country. We were unaware of the impending change until Val's eleventh birthday when Mummy told her she was going to Loreto Abbey Rathfarnham in Dublin as a boarder in September of that year. The gentle cocoon of growing up in Drogheda was broken.

An Roinn Oideachais
Brainse an Bunoideachais

Teistiméireacht ar Bunoideachas

Dearbú é seo gur críochnaigh _Valerie Ní Ceasain_ an séú rang de chlár an teagaisc sna scoileanna náisiúnta agus gur éirigh leis an dalta san sa scrúdú scríofa sa Ghaeilge, sa Bhéarla agus san uimhríocht a tionóladh ag an Roinn Oideachais i mí an Mheithimh, 1959, le haghaidh na Teistiméireachta ar Bunoideachas.

T. Ó Raifeartaigh
Rúnaí

Is iad seo leanas na hábhair de chlár an teagaisc atá ordaithe le haghaidh an tséú rang i scoileanna náisiúnta:—

Ábair Éigeantacha:
Gaeilge, Béarla, matamaitic, stair, tíreolaíocht, ceol, obair shnáthaide (Cailíní).

Ábair Neamhéigeantacha:
líníocht, corpoiliúint, tuaiteolaíocht nó eolas ar nádúr, cócaireacht (Cailíní), níocán (Cailíní), nó tíos (Cailíní), lámhoiliúint (buachaillí).

Ionad. 30018

Valerie's National Primary Exam Certificate.
She passed the obligatory subjects: Irish (Gaelic), English, Mathematics, History, Geography, Music and Sewing (girls only).

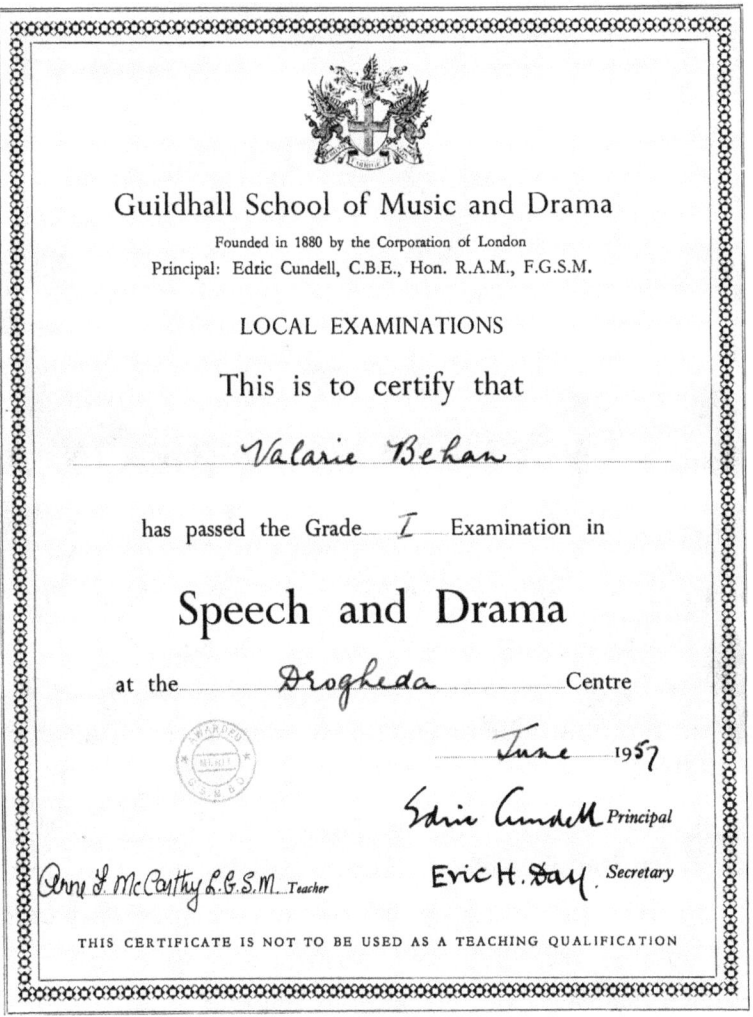

Elocution was taken seriously at St. Philomena's. Under Miss McCarthy's watchful eye, Valerie passed Grade I exam in Speech and Drama.

Loreto Abbey Rathfarnham

Loreto Abbey Rathfarnham was the Mother House of the Irish branch of The Sisters of Loreto, an order of nuns founded by Mary Ward in 1609. For her time, Mary Ward was unusual; she believed that women were equal to men in intellect and should be educated accordingly. She was a woman after our mother's heart. She followed the thinking and principles of St. Ignatius of Loyola who founded the Jesuits, and applied these concepts to women, establishing her religious institute and opening schools for girls. She envisioned women living a religious life in companionship and discernment, engaging with the world without the constraints of the traditional cloister, and without being subservient to the local male clergy. Her ideas were radical, and because they were linked to those of the Jesuits, her religious institute suffered repeated suppression during the next hundred years. It did not receive papal recognition as a religious institute until 1877. It was called The Institute of the Blessed Virgin Mary.

The Irish branch of this order of nuns was founded by Sister Francis Mary Theresa Ball in Dublin in 1847. Frances Ball was born into a wealthy, Catholic family at a time when Catholicism was suppressed in Ireland. She was sent to the Bar Convent in York, a Sisters of Loreto School, to be educated. Frances returned to Dublin when she was sixteen; she is described as talented and striking. She was expected to make an exceptional wife, but instead, with the encouragement of Archbishop Murray of Dublin, she returned to the Bar Convent for religious training. She took the religious name of Teresa, returned to Dublin in 1823 and began to set up the Irish branch of the order, with the mother house being at Loreto Abbey Rathfarnham. Over the next forty years she established a wide network of convents and schools across Ireland, as well as in India, Mauritius and Canada. She died in 1861, by which time she had founded thirty-seven convents in various parts of the world.

During our years at the Abbey (1959—1967), the school was considered among the best secondary schools in Ireland, if not the best. What was meant by "best"? Abbey girls were educated to go to university or pursue other areas of higher education, to take on civic responsibilities as educators, councilors and mayors, to demonstrate independence and intellectual rigor, to live up to their parents' and the nuns' expectations of them, and to never forget that they were "Abbey Girls." The Abbey was also considered among the strictest boarding schools in Ireland. We went to school for the autumn term in September and did not get out until the Christmas holidays. We could not go home at weekends. Similarly, we returned to school in January, and except for a ten day Easter holiday, we did not go home again until early June.

The Loreto nuns were themselves educated Irish women from backgrounds undoubtedly similar to our own. They were strict, but generally kind. We suffered no physical or sexual abuse. Granted we were lonely, home-sick, bored and rebellious at times, but the nuns tried to dispel these feelings by filling every moment with some kind of activity: class, study, chapel, music, plays, sports, all interspersed with regular and nourishing (if uninspiring) meals.

We Behan girls owe the nuns an enormous debt; they helped make us the successful professional women we became. Like the nuns who taught us, we have no children of our own, but we both became educators. Our students became our children and hopefully we have paid forward the debt we owe Loreto Abbey Rathfarnham.

Loreto Abbey Rathfarnham

Part 2: The Abbey

Arrival

Dear Mary,

    Do you remember the beginning, not the first day, but when you were told you were going to boarding school? Mummy must have told me just after my eleventh birthday. She said I was going to Loreto Abbey Rathfarnham, the best boarding school in Ireland, her speak for the most graduates going to university, and not to worry because GC was there and would 'look out for me.' GC was two years older than I, and an acquaintance not a friend. None of my friends was going there, but this was equivalent to a papal decree. I suppose it became more real when Mummy came into my bedroom and gave me a novel to read saying 'this will tell you what boarding school is really like.' Ah, I so wish I could remember the name of this book! I do remember that it had more hefty emotions in it than I was used to, with girls clustering in malevolent cliques and hockey sticks clashing. It didn't end happily.

Of course, I thought boarding school would be like it was in the comics, the ones in which girls formed happy cliques, played loads of games, didn't have to work hard and there was just one girl whom nobody liked, but everything ended happily. Those were the comics I had borrowed from Margaret O'Kane and the McAuleys. Did Mummy buy us comics — I don't think so — or maybe one each? We really depended on the O'Kanes and the McAuleys for comic fodder. Wasn't that the most wonderful path, the one going out the back at Green Gables, through our orchard to 'Daddy Gauleys'? There was a wilderness of grass and nettles and wildflowers in spring and summer and then one of the locals, or Dad, would scythe the orchard and the world changed. We could see the heaped circles of plaster of Paris impressions for false teeth that Dad used as fertilizer around the base of the apple trees. We'd slip along the path on a Saturday and Sunday morning, and if Daddy Gauley was making breakfast for Carmel and Gabriel he would include us and we would have sinfully smashing rashers and sausages, and sometimes black pudding. Carmel and Gabriel got loads of comics including the young teenager variety.

I don't know when the 'List' arrived of all the items that I needed for boarding school: the engraved cutlery, the sheets, towels, face cloth, and all the clothing, the blouses, pinafores, vests, panties, socks. Everything needed my name sewn on, and when the name tabs came I remember Mummy being not too excited by the sewing on business. It was not her forte, and we didn't have a sewing machine. Of course these weren't items from any random source; they had to be purchased at Clerys in Dublin. What did parents do if they lived in Mayo or Donegal? Now you would think a day spent in Clerys totally devoted to getting me set for school would be exciting, but it only confirmed that I was a very big girl for eleven. I think they had to search in the women's shoes section for size 41 brogues for me!

I have blanked the time between Clerys and the final day. I must have had a normal summer, but my life would not be free in boarding school, no biking wherever I wanted after doing homework, no wandering, climbing trees, or playing tennis when I wanted. What I remember is the drive from Drogheda to Dublin, playing games with God that he would ordain a benign accident, a flat tire, there would be a traffic jam, anything to delay arrival. When we reached Harold's Cross I wanted time to stand still, I wanted that drive to slow down infinitely; what was the use of physics if it couldn't delay arrival at boarding school? I dreaded the saying goodbye, and the choked tears. I know we arrived during the afternoon the first time, and that it was sunny and that the nuns looked benevolent. But it is always the Gormenghast way in my dreams — arriving in rainy darkness. I don't think you came with me that first time.

Dear Val,

I'm not certain whether I came with you the first

time. Probably I was left at home with our housekeeper Alice, Mummy fearing that there would be a show of tears from someone. Definitely not her — tears would never have been allowed. But Daddy would have cried quietly. Based on what I remember from subsequent 'first evenings,' the drill was to deposit the trunk at the side door near the gym, and proceed up the main outside staircase to the hall door. I expect that new girls were deftly separated from their parents who would have been ushered back to the four corners of the country with a firm 'safe journey now,' and a rapid door closing. The hapless newcomer would then be delivered to an older pupil, likely a Prefect, and sorted out as to where they would be sleeping. Because I arrived with you my first time, there was no front door meet and greet. Rather, we both were dropped at the side door with our luggage, with the expectation that you would look after me. There was no possibility of me crying — I couldn't wait to start boarding school!

We dragged our trunks to a spot along the corridor that linked the refectory to the cloakroom and classroom wing, and unpacked them there. I can still smell the disinfectant. It was simmering away in a black pot, perched on a primus stove on the floor. What were they trying to kill? True, the cloakroom, with years of accumulated damp, held at least 150 pairs of smelly, canvas and rubber hockey boots. That, combined with the germs that 150 girls were bringing from the outside after weeks of unencumbered play — it's no wonder the nuns felt that they needed the disinfectant!

Next came the task of finding out where you were

sleeping that year. Sometimes a nun would remember your dormitory assignment, but generally you could guess and run upstairs quickly to check. Novices were stationed in each dorm to point you to your cubicle. After that we carried the contents of our trunk, armful by armful, to our bedside lockers and moved in.

That first September you brought me to St. Teresa's dormitory, made sure I had a cubicle with my name on it, and left me to my own devices. I didn't mind. Everything was new and exciting and I couldn't wait to get organized and meet my neighbors who were all going to be in Grade One with me. There were four girls from Drogheda at the Abbey besides us, and one of them was in my class. JM and I had been in St. Philomena's Junior School together, although we weren't close friends at the time. Still, any familiar face was welcome those first few weeks at the Abbey.

For the first time in my life I had a suite of crisp, new clothes. I had grown accustomed to hand-me-downs from you, but I honestly think that however much Mummy hated sewing nametags on any garment, she drew the line at first having to remove an old tag before sewing on a new one. So I got everything new.

Empty trunks were dragged to the trunk room presided over by Mother Attracta. Because of listening to you for two years, I knew all the nicknames for nuns. She was 'Tractor,' although she seemed too old to merit a nickname. Trunks were arrayed around the room on shelves, and remained there until the Christmas holidays. On trips to Mother Attracta's 'emporium' during the term, we would look longingly at our trunk, reminding ourselves that the holidays would come eventually.

On that first evening there was a lovely sense of chaos, chatter, excitement and discovery. The default rule of Silence hadn't been explained to us as yet, and there was little point in admonishing anyone for running on the corridors while they were getting settled in. All of that would come later.

We always went back to school in the evening after tea. What did they give us before going to bed? A hot drink I suppose. Then a bell rang to signify that it was time to go to our dormitories. We all made our beds, and then pulled the curtains of our cubicles closed. 'Home' was a metal frame bed, a locker and a chair. On top of the locker was a basin and jug of water, soap dish and a glass. I remember putting on my new pajamas and dressing gown, brushing my teeth, and climbing into a strange bed where I had new sheets with my name on them! Mother Fidelis said a prayer and a few of us muttered 'Amen.' Then the lights went out.

THE REFECTORY

Dear Val,

I was thinking about letters at the Abbey the other day. They were delivered in the refectory, which itself conjures up a host of different memories. We used to call it the 'refetry' with an emphasis on the first syllable. Of course we knew how to spell and pronounce the word correctly: r-e-f-e-c-t-o-r-y. Mother Emmanuel who taught us English, would never have it otherwise. Still, saying it this way demonstrated a particular familiarity. After all, it was an anchor to the day, complete with distinct smells that were the harbinger of plentiful, but mostly uninspired, unappetizing food. Once we had canned peas twenty-seven days in a row, delivered in what we were sure were recycled German World War II helmets. They were strikingly ugly but durable, probably similar to our concept of Germans, until we met them later in our teens as deprived, young Irish virgins and concluded otherwise. At any rate, letters were delivered during mealtimes. We went to the refectory four times day, in silence, in single file. We could have been coming from the chapel or the classroom, but it was always in silence. Now, fifty years later, I recognize that there is a lot to be said for silence. But then it was strange. Remember, we were in a convent that housed as many nuns as there were pupils. These nuns were young, middle-aged, old, retired, vacationing, visiting from the Indian and African missions, and some of them had left the bounds of reality. Combine these with 150 girls aged eleven to eighteen, and you have a biologically significant collection of womanhood and sex hormones!

We filed into the refectory at 12:30 each day and stood behind our respective chairs waiting for the bell, rather like Pavlov's dogs. Our life was controlled by bells. Indeed, one of the most cherished 'honors' was to be given the responsibility of ringing those bells. You got the freedom to leave every event slightly early, poised, waiting for that powerful moment when you could quite literally move everyone in your world.

A single nun presided over the meal, seated on a dais at the top of the room. She didn't eat (I never thought about that at the time, but then again, it wasn't much of a gastric sacrifice, I'm sure). She said grace ('Bless me Father and these thy gifts which of thy bounty we are about to receive through Christ Our Lord,' to which we all dutifully replied, 'Amen'), and we all sat down, in silence, waiting for the bell. When it rang, conversation erupted. And so the meal progressed. This was our main meal of the day: watery *soup, meat, vegetable and potato, followed by dessert. During dessert, letters were distributed. Mother Consiglio or Mother Fidelis or Mother…whomever was in charge that day, would glide around the room handing out mail over our shoulders, while we pretended not to expect or hope or wish or pray, or dream of getting anything. We all were hoping for a letter, always. It might be your parents, but it just might be your 'brother' signing off affectionately. With little or no contact with boys while we were at the Abbey, we all acquired brothers (otherwise known as boyfriends), who wrote politely but irregularly.*

As I remember this now, I was struck by the fact that we had no need to tear the envelopes open. All of our mail was opened, and by assumption, pre-read. Now, many years later, I pity the nun who had to screen the correspondence. It must have been an emotionally taxing job: to try to protect each and every one of us from things that she might never have experienced, but had some inkling could do us harm such as sickness, death, unhappiness, depression, alcoholism, infidelity, financial troubles. What an impossible task! Not even God could have been much use to her.

And as for the letters themselves…well, Mummy wrote religiously every week. I don't remember one word that she wrote. I just remember her amazing handwriting — distinctive and confident, and weird. Her loops and 'g's were fabulous, if not extraordinary. Equally comforting is the absence of a memory of unhappiness in her letters. And as for Daddy — did we ever get letters from him? Maybe from when they went on holiday abroad, but I'm not sure. Nor do I remember the logistics of shared letters. Were they addressed to you one week and me the next, or did Mummy write to both of us each week? Were we allowed get up from our places in the refectory without asking permission and give a letter to a sibling, for random movement was tightly controlled, rather like movement in a contemporary prison.

And what happened to those letters? Were I to read them now, would they tell me more about our dead parents and their relationship? Or would they trigger other sleepy neural circuits in the recesses of my brain telling me about a younger me?

Dear Mary,

What a vivid picture of the 'refetry,' and of course it sounds much more organized than I remember it. I think that over the years the Abbey's refectory has got mixed up with other refectory-like conditions, such as the many dining halls along the Alaskan pipeline, or at various universities. But you are so right — the Abbey was special. I don't remember the peas, but I vividly remember dessert, especially the execrable roly-poly. It was a bread pudding with a jam sauce, and was sweet, but it stuck to the roof of your mouth like a paste, and we seemed to get it at least three times a week. I do remember it twice in a row a good few times, for which I'm loath to forgive God. My favorite dessert was the milky coffee with Kimberley biscuits which we got about once a fortnight. I think we got 3 biscuits each, but occasionally a pupil would be absent, and they would forget to take it into account. Were the other type of biscuits the coconut cream puffs, or were those the ones we got from Mummy when she came to visit? In retrospect, biscuits were the high-point of the questionable culinary delights that the Abbey provided. Of course, Kimberley biscuits have never tasted so good since.

Funny I don't remember much about letters, other than that they were opened, but I lived in fear of getting one from the Loreto missions saying that I was accepted for some overseas jihad. You see, LR, who sat beside me in Study, and who was way too bright for the small amount of homework we were given, would write letters on my behalf, and without my knowledge, to the Total Abstinence crowd (who were they?) saying how I was driven with love of Mary to bring purity, chastity and abstinence to…well, to whomever needed it.

The whole letter business helped teach me how to dissemble. Do you remember poor GC who got a letter from a boyfriend in Grade Six, and the numbskull did not hide his identity as a 'brother,' and sent her love and perhaps even kisses. Her letter was read out in the refectory to all of us as an example of perdition. I think most of us just took it to heart as an example of how stupid we would never be.

Mostly though I remember glorious birthdays in the refectory. Where did the cakes come from? There must have been a standing order with some bakery because they looked similar and had mounds of pink, mauve and orangy-red icing — you know the stuff that is hard to the touch but melts in your mouth, and that probably left us with a life-time supply of toxins. But who cares. And I remember tea, especially on a Sunday. If Mummy had visited us that day, we got a cake or biscuits to share. And if Dad had visited, the bag of windfall apples he brought didn't go down too well. Parents of the Dublin pupils always visited and always brought cake or whatever, and we had our fill at tea that evening. One time a girl got two cakes — I still remember the orgy of icing. Best of all, in our final year LR's Mummy always left the Sunday Times Magazine with her pile of goodies, and I got it eventually. That's how I knew about fashion photographers and models, and advertisements and layout — bliss.

But we didn't say grace at every meal — did we? I thought the afternoon snack (or whatever it was called) was a free for all. One term, crusts were all the rage and sixth years would dash in ahead of others to the refectory and swipe the crusts from as many tables as possible. As you were younger, you probably never got to eat crusts!

Dear Val,

I was thinking about our meals at the Abbey. They were probably fairly balanced, if a bit heavy on carbohydrates. I don't remember anyone being a picky eater either. You just ate what was on the table, and as much or little of it as you wanted. Some girls were thin, and others plump. But the majority seemed pretty average in size. Could bulimia and anorexia have existed and we just didn't notice? Body image is hard to focus on when there are no mirrors! There was a mirror over each sink in the dormitories, but with that many girls emptying basins of water and filling jugs, or brushing their teeth, nobody could linger to admire themself. There was one full-length mirror at the end of the Gallery in the classroom wing, just outside the Domestic Science sewing room. But again, you never lingered because a nun could appear at any moment and interrogate you as to what you were doing, or where you were going.

Breakfast consisted of as much tea, bread and butter as you wanted. Big bowls of cornflakes were laid out for us to help ourselves. On alternate days, those German helmets appeared again, this time filled with a glutinous porridge that could probably have held bricks together. The butter was carved into star-shaped patties, which I always thought was very civilized. Some years later when I had a chance to see the inside of Sister Colette's kitchen, I realized that they just squished all the scraped-off plates of butter from the last meal into a machine, and hand cranked it to generate the next plate of patties. Some people got hard-boiled eggs, an 'extra' that presumably had to be paid for separately by their parents. There was no such thing as a soft-boiled egg, or any other sort of egg for that matter, and rashers didn't exist for love or money.

The main course at mid-day dinner was always thin brown soup followed by boiled beef or mutton, boiled potatoes, and a vegetable, invariably cabbage, peas or turnips. As for desserts, roly-poly wasn't one of my favorites either. I came across a description of something like it recently, in one of Patrick O'Brien's (Aubrey & Maturin) novels, set on a British Naval vessel in the early 1800s. Mummy got it too when she was at boarding school at Kylemore Abbey, and they used to call it 'boiled baby'! Another dessert we got was yellow or green jelly with slices of banana floating in it like insects caught forever in amber. And then there were prunes. I suppose they worked. I never remember being constipated. But then again, I didn't know what it was to be constipated. I didn't know anything about how my body worked, although I knew that peanut butter was banned by the nuns because it caused appendicitis! Other food substances like Ketchup were banned too, probably for the same 'sound' medical reasons.

I think the afternoon collation was called 'Lunch,' an afternoon tea of sorts. It happened around 4:00 when classes had finished, and consisted of tea, bread and butter, and whatever fruit and jam our families had brought as presents. The latter were stored in big cardboard boxes that were deposited at each table in the refectory and doled out by us. Did we share or trade? Probably a little of both. After that we trooped to the cloakroom, changed into hockey boots or tennis shoes depending on the term, and went out, hail, rain or snow, for half an hour of vigorous exercise. It was a relief to come back in at 5:00 for Study, a quiet couple of hours punctuated only by a change in the presiding nun, or a bathroom break (hand raised to ask permission, of course). At 7:00 we went to chapel for prayers, and at 7:30 we filed into the refectory once again for Tea. This was my favorite meal. You never knew what would appear. There was the ubiquitous tea, bread and butter, of course. (I often think that the nuns were way ahead of their time in terms of being eco-friendly. Those mountains of waste tealeaves were used to sweep all the floors in the school — a great way to collect dust and maintain a patina on the hardwood floors). There could also be lettuce and hard-boiled eggs with Heinz Salad Cream, or maybe plates of sliced ham. What else did we get? I can't believe that I don't remember. I do remember that on Wednesdays and Sundays we got our own cakes and biscuits, once again delivered in cardboard boxes for us to dole out to ourselves, and if there was enough, to share with other girls at the same table.

On your birthday, regardless of what day of the week it was, you got the cake your parents baked, or arranged to have delivered to the school. It was expected that you would share it with your table and your class. And best of all, if it was your sister's birthday (she being in another class at another table), you got a slice too, while everybody else at your table drooled with envy because birthday cakes were always very good. Various Dublin bakeries came and went as favorite sources for birthday treats. Do you remember cakes from Teatime Express and Bewleys, and Fuller's 'Bombs': glorious, cream-filled choux pastries covered with chocolate or coffee icing?

CHAPEL

Dear Val,

The chapel was a beautiful place: serene, with a lingering scent of incense and beeswax candles. Have you noticed that whenever you smell either of these nowadays, it's like a shot of yoga breathing — everything calms down and the world seems to be a better place. Maybe aromatherapy isn't such bunk after all. We'd line up in the dormitory and march down in a single file, in silence of course, to morning Mass. Prefects were stationed at corners, the top of staircases, in doorways. I've no idea why. We were barely awake and headed for the chapel like zombies. Did we have assigned seating in the chapel? The three nuns who were head of First, Second and Third Schools knelt in prie-dieux at the back of our wing of the chapel, alert to our shenanigans. But that early in the morning we were pretty subdued.

The chapel as seen from the nuns' perspective with their individual prie-dieux. Girls were to the left of the altar (not visible) and Lay Sisters to the right (also not visible).

It just struck me, as I thought of chapel, that we had to wear veils. How did we manage to keep our veils at hand? Considering we went to chapel two or three times a day, that veil must have been attached to us by a leash. I cannot see you thinking to yourself as you left Study in the evening: 'I must remember to take my veil to the dormitory with me.' Actually, knowing you, you would have used it as an excuse to rush back there before lights-out and read a novel for a few extra minutes!

Dark-haired Father Sullivan and two pimply boys would strut onto the altar by 7:05. Everyone was already in their places. The Lay Sisters were huddled in black masses in the wing opposite us. They had regular benches like us, unlike the nuns who entered the convent with dowries and had individual prie-dieux in the nave of the chapel. Despite wearing approximately the same habit, we always knew who was a Lay Sister and who was not. Why was that? Did they not have a white bib (which would have been guaranteed to get dirty with cooking and cleaning), or was it their demeanor? We all knelt in silence and waited for Mass to begin.

How many'of us were there? Say 150 girls, maybe 50 Lay Sisters, and another 100 or more nuns. The numbers changed when nuns came back from the missions for their holidays, or when we got new Postulants. The latter were fascinating — barely older than us, wearing a habit halfway between nun and schoolgirl: a three-quarter length skirt, a navy cardigan over a white blouse, but no tie. And their hair was still there. Actually, some still had their nail polish intact. Do you remember that we used to take bets as to whether they would outlast their last manicure? After about six months a Postulant would metamorphose into a Novice, with hair hidden, and dressed in a long habit. But they still looked different from real nuns. What was it that distinguished them? Certainly the Novices were softer, gentler, and unsure of themselves in the same way that baby priests are. They seemed to spend inordinate hours hand weaving a crios (that woven belt that St. Francis of Assisi is always shown wearing), with little balls of yarn dangling from their busy fingers. There are elements of a Grimm fairy tale here: weaving something endlessly while waiting, waiting…and the resulting object never seems to show any sign of progress or completion.

Everyone took Communion. That must have passed the time for us, hungry, waiting to be released to breakfast. There was such a pecking order: nuns first, then us, then the Lay Sisters. Everyone filed out of chapel in pecking order too. But I think they must have let the Lay Sisters go early so that they could get breakfast going for us. Or maybe Sister Colette left early. Do you remember Sister Colette? She was in charge of the refectory and was a sweetie. I remember her as always looking hot and flushed. Mind you, she probably was, supervising meals for 300 people three times a day. Then again, it could have been menopause. We never had a clue what age a nun was. Once they took their final vows (when they were likely to be around 25 years old), they entered into that zone of agelessness. Without hair or makeup clues, we weren't clever enough to look at hands or laugh lines. Actually, I don't think we would have believed that they could develop laugh lines, with a couple of exceptions. But going by the numbers, there must have been thirty or more women going through menopause in the Abbey at any one time. What a concept!

Dear Mary,

But you know Mass was a joy (well maybe not the second one in the same day) mainly because of the chapel. It was so lovely, beautifully proportioned, graceful, creamy white and even though our stomachs were constantly growling, and there was more than a bit of routine about it, I think we were all calm in chapel. And then there was the yearly anticipation as to what the altar boys would look like. There were usually three, I remember three dark-haired, good-looking boys one year. I think when my hormones were developing there were three plain red-heads with pimply faces. We all agreed they had a high 'yuck' factor. Amazing that we remember them so clearly, but of course they were the only males in our world. Nobody's brothers came to the Parlour for visits, and other male relatives were extraordinarily rare. Those altar boys must have been trained within an inch of their lives; they never messed up and always had the correct sequence of chalice and those dipping things. They swung the thurible strongly enough to smell the chapel out. Actually now that I think of it, it was probably to cover up the smell of over 100 male-deprived young females, and even more nuns. And they helped with communion without once leering at any of us — or did they? I wasn't the type to warrant leers.

And then there were the High Masses. When did we have those? I know there was one coming up to Christmas and one in May. We got a chance to sing at High Mass — now that was glorious. Do you remember singing masses in Gregorian chant, and we had one by Mendelssohn or was it one of the other great M's, that I loved. We practiced for days and weeks and then it would all happen just once. That seemed so unfair. Mother Philippa (Pip) would pound the chapel organ and voices soared. I'm sure they did, even mine and I couldn't sing a note in tune, though I was 'on chord.'

The chapel had beautiful side altars. The confessional was beside one of them. We were meant to come out suitably penitent and pray at one of the side altars until we were reposed enough to return to class to sin again. To be honest, what did we tell the priest in confessional and how could any of us really sin at boarding school? Okay, we could be mean, or think and speak badly of someone, but we were too cowed to swear, too well brought up to steal (and what would you steal?) and too exhausted to have bad thoughts. We must have been such a disappointment for the priests who led the annual Retreat, especially the 'fire and brimstone' types. Remember the year we had the Pauline Brothers, or was it the year of the John of Gods? I think I was thirteen or fourteen and I didn't understand the half of their preaching, and they went on spouting fire and brimstone for well over an hour for each session. Of course we couldn't talk to each other as we were in Retreat for three days. I think they were repressed, or assumed that we were sex crazed maniacs constantly self-titillating. At least that is what their questions in the confessional implied. Some of the senior girls were in tears leaving the confessional. I think there was a 'word said' because we never saw that Order of priests again. That's my only negative memory of chapel and the only Retreat that wasn't wonderful.

Returning from Confession

Dormitory Life

Dear Val,

Your description of the first day got me thinking about how we knew anything at all of how things worked at boarding school. Who showed you what to do? At least I had you, whether you liked it or not. For the previous two years I had been hearing all about the Abbey, and couldn't wait to get there. It sounded so exciting, like the 'Famous Five' or 'Secret Seven' in Enid Blyton's books, my only reading besides comics. By the way, we did get the Beano comic occasionally. I begged to have a subscription, and Mummy might have given in for a few months, but I'm sure she despaired of its tattiness and decided to quit.

I watched Mummy sew my nametags on to everything. They were called Cash's marks. Not surprisingly, I loved having my own stuff. My engraved silverware was beautiful, even though the letters were in regular uppercase, not like yours, which were in italics. I was a bit jealous. Auntie Anne had made bags for us with the word 'Laundry' embroidered diagonally across the front in blue. Remember all those times you were forced to accompany me to the toilet at home in Greenhills? I used to be terrified of the strange noise that the flush sometimes made, imagining a jaguar leaping out of the cistern. You would hiss at me in disgust, saying that I couldn't be doing this at boarding school! No wonder you wanted to distance yourself from me in those early years.

That first morning I remember a disembodied arm coming through the curtains of my cubicle, and a low voice intoning 'Benedicamus dominum.' Actually, I had no idea what the nun said, or even that it was a nun's arm. The hand was carrying a small bowl of water, definitely too small to take and wash in, and it didn't seem the sort you drank out of. Eventually the bowl was waved at me (I'm still hidden behind the curtain), and I got it: it was holy water! I was meant to dip my finger in it, make the sign of the cross and recite 'Amen.' The nuns must have been so frustrated with our ignorance at the beginning — we were clueless first years and had nobody around us to copy.

Mother Fidelis presided over St. Teresa's dormitory. She was tall, beautiful and had a radiant smile. I thought she was the embodiment of an angel (well, maybe a little too tall), and she absolutely glided around in her black habit. She was in charge of first and second year pupils (which made up the Third School), a bit like Maggie Smith in the Harry Potter movies. Remember, we called her Fido. All the nuns had nicknames, and most of the girls too. Four days a week we woke at 6:30 for Mass at 7:00. There would be the round of 'Benedicamus dominum,' and then a few minutes later the sound of washing. With a jug of cold water and a basin, the wash was pretty cursory I'm sure. At that age we didn't know about smelly underarms or pudenda, so perhaps only our face got a lick. Clad in pyjamas or nighties and wooly dressing gowns, we'd empty the basins at the sinks that were down a few steps at the end of the dormitory, the scene of many unfortunate, wet accidents to everyone's joy. We'd make one more trip to brush our teeth at the sinks, and maybe a trip to one of the two toilets that were shared by dozens of girls. Before leaving our cubicles, we had to strip the bed. I remember distinctly the six blankets on our beds, so threadbare that you might as well have not bothered. They must have been in use since the Abbey first opened in the 1800s. Most of us cheated and lifted everything as a unit, sheet, blankets and bedspread (also threadbare). But occasionally we'd be pointed out for our laziness, and made to separate them into a huge unruly pile on the chair, to be made up after Mass and breakfast. Then we'd file out of the dormitory, down endless corridors and stairs to the chapel, bleary eyed, with veils perched on our heads.

Mother Fidelis had a curtained cubicle like the rest of us, but hers was larger and the curtains always stayed closed. She had windows too. All of us were fascinated as to what she wore, and would watch the shadowy shapes on the ceiling as she undressed by candlelight. The big questions were about breasts and hair. Did nuns have any of either? Were breasts squashed, and if so, with what?

How short was their hair, or were they bald? What did their underwear look like? Did they use a suspender belt to hold up their stockings?

Dear Mary,

Yes, how did we know? There was no 'Loreto One' mimicking 'Law One,' or the OSHA guide to clean living. I know somehow we lugged our clothes up to St. Teresa's and I suppose, a bit like receiving the Holy Ghost, knowledge arrived. My cell was further along to the right than yours, and so it was easier to see the nightly shapes of the nun (it wasn't Mother Fidelis at that time) who occupied the corner cell. But I recall no breasts, or unsightly removal of garments over her head.

Ah, the 'Benedicamus Dominum.' I think the first morning the disembodied arm may have given us a hint of what to do, though I'm not sure, as there was meant to be no talking before Mass. I was the 'arm with the holy water and the low voice' in Grade Five and Six I think. In Grade Six we seniors were in our own rooms, but we were still meant to leap out of bed at the morning bell and be waiting for the arm. The bell would ring and I'd leap out of bed (after my five years of leaping-in-training I was good at this), and grab the holy water container (a glass jar I remember). Then came the negotiations with those in the other rooms — 'It's okay Valerie, I'm awake' being the common response to 'Benedicamus Dominum.' Needless to say there was no gentle pressure on the jar as they turned over in bed and went back to sleep. I usually compromised and left them alone, as I had to do these rounds before getting myself washed and dressed for Mass.

Dear Val,

There weren't many ways to achieve status at the Abbey. Being good at sports was one, and we worshipped the Games Captain from afar, for the first few years at least. Being a Prefect was another status point. After that, the only thing that made you feel special (or not) was the dormitory to which you were assigned. I doubt that the nuns lost any sleep over these assignments, but I certainly did. I dreaded being sent back to St. Anne's in Grade Five.

Grade One was easy. Everyone was put in St. Teresa's under the watchful eye of Fido. And if there were a few too many, the adjacent smaller rooms also had cubicles. What were those rooms called? They were a little nicer than St. Teresa's, with the chance of getting a window. Also, they didn't have a resident nun. But you still washed in a basin of cold water, and refilled your jug from the communal taps at the bottom of the steps in St. Teresa's. Do you remember that we were all lined up once a month to get a tablespoon of syrup of figs, no doubt because someone hadn't responded appropriately to the weekly prunes.

Where did we sleep in Grade Two? Grade Three was my best year by far. I got to share a room with you in St. Joseph's. There were about seven small rooms in an attic above the concert hall. Each had a tiny dormer window that opened, and you felt like you were 'sur les toits de Paris' even if you were only looking out on the front lawn and the chapel. In the distance we could see the Dublin Mountains. The room we shared was number five, down the corridor towards the end on the left. Mother Ailbe had a room there too. We never came up with a good nickname for her. She was terrifying, and had hairs on her chin — a nun version of Darth Vader. The beds and lockers and blankets were the same as in St. Teresa's, but I think we had a sink with lukewarm water. It seemed so spacious and private after the curtained cubicles, although you couldn't lock the door. On Saturday mornings a Novice would check that everything in our locker was in order before combing our hair and checking our fingernails. But besides that (and the 'Benedicamus Dominum' each morning after a knock on the door), we were alone. Still, I have no memory of any conversation you and I might have had there. Do you?

Grade Four was my nemesis. I fully expected that as you were Head Girl, we would be given the best room on the floor above the gym — Lisieux was the name of it, I think. But no. Nuns were forever getting in the way of my view of how the world should work, and they decided that you should have a room of your own. I had to join the lumpen-proletariat in the horseboxes of St. Anne's. At least I had half a window; the other half was in KH's cubicle. There was a gap between the wooden partition and the window, and we exchanged lots of things across that gap which, unlike the space between the partition and the floor, couldn't be monitored by a nun. This sounds so paranoid as I write it now, but we attributed amazing, prescient powers to nuns. So that year it was back to the basin and jug routine in St. Anne's, back to the ever-present nun in a corner cubicle, and her shadow on the ceiling after lights out.

I got back to St. Joseph's in Grade Five. For once the Gods smiled favorably down upon me and I was assigned a room with JM and BM, both in my class. Ah — that was a great year: we felt so adult at fifteen or sixteen, and I suppose we were. You had gone to university and I was on my own. Did I miss you? A little — but you were more useful to me on the outside. Besides, I was a Prefect and doing well academically (spurred, no doubt, by a long-standing rivalry with MM, MC and EH). My room-mates were both brilliant at sports (they later became Games Captain and Vice-Captain), so I felt well-connected and 'in' on everything of importance.

All Grade Six got their own room, or shared with one or two others in Lisieux or St. Cecelia's above the gym. Those were lovely rooms, and they had hot water. The only downside was that they also served as music practice rooms for everyone. You never knew who had looked over your stuff, checked out your ornaments (we were only allowed one or two), or investigated your photographs (again, only allowed one or two). We couldn't hang anything on the walls either. Do you remember, inside every room was a holy water font. I wonder where the nuns got all the water they needed to fill those fonts? There must have been hundreds scattered around the Abbey. Did they present Father Sullivan with gallon jugs and ask him to bless them?

ABBEY GIRLS

Dear Mary,

Ah now! St. Anne's wasn't too bad, and it was infinitely better than St. Teresa's. At least we had the horse stables effect and so had some privacy on three sides. I was used to only sharing a room with you at home, so I can tell you St. Teresa's was a shock with just flimsy curtains between us and another pupil on either side, and many others across the open space of the dorm. At least we had curtains; I think boarders at boy schools had no privacy at all. Of course, as we were newcomers in St. Teresa's dormitory, no thought was given to our placement. I would definitely have liked to be closer to the toilets because even at that age, I had a mouse-sized bladder. Do you remember waking up wanting to go to the toilet, but wondering was it worth it given that that bell for Mass would be going off soon, but without a watch you didn't quite know when. So many of us were homesick in St. Teresa's. I remember one of the Lebanese pupils who was much younger than us crying herself to sleep in the next cubicle, and not being able to do anything about it. No sympathy or empathy was allowed after lights-out; we had said our 'Amen' and should be asleep.

So St. Anne's seemed an enormous improvement in the second year. I didn't have a window, but I had one of the stalls close to the door and therefore, close to the toilets. Maybe that's why St. Anne's is always a bright place in my memory. And we kept the same stall for the terms and years we were there, in my case 2 years. So it was like your own tent in the barrenness of the Arctic — it was yours, it was home. Not that there was anything personal in this stall, no photos of parents or whatever dog we had at home, no books; we kept everything, especially our dreams, tucked away in our 'memory palaces.'

St. Joseph's was wonderful. Sharing a room with you was what we had done at home, so it felt normal. Other than the Novice who checked our small locker for poorly folded clothes, and the floor for dust bunnies, it was our demesne. On a moonlight night there was enough light to read, hanging out the window; I remember studying trigonometry for an exam that way. The space was probably smaller than two St. Anne stalls, but the luxurious privacy was incomparable. In retrospect, St. Joseph's was much better than my accommodation in Grade Six. Granted, as Head Girl, I had the best single room, and the taps produced hot water, and the room had a decent window, but it had that piano for girls' practicing, and so lacked the privacy of St. Joseph's. I think there was a toilet on the stairs on the way to the top floor and St. Joseph's, no closer. Still, no one was going to lug a piano up those stairs.

NUNS

Dear Mary,

    And you ask: why 'Abbey Girls'? We were always 'the girls' to Daddy and Mummy. But for six years of our lives we were 'Loreto girls,' more specifically 'Abbey girls' and so the best of the best. I was thinking that perhaps we never stop being Abbey girls, as it changed us forever. We had remarkable teachers, cultured women who were dedicated to forming us into the kind of women who could meet any challenge, and be ambitious, assertive, outspoken leaders.

    I think partly it was the surroundings; the Abbey was a beautiful school, with its wedding-cake chapel, elegant central building, interesting architecture and lovely grounds. Think of the pond with its two swans, surrounded by trees and shrubs and the glorious central walk by the majestic chestnut trees. We had the two field hockey pitches, the netball and tennis courts, the long walk through the gardens, and all protected by a high wall. And in front we had those graceful lawns sweeping down to the main gate. I think the ambiance helped in later life — we had lived in beauty, knew what architecture could be, knew the calming value of space. And of course that shows in the spaces where we have ended up living.

I know that we learned the value of broad friendship with girls from backgrounds and countries different from ours. We learned collaboration, the value of helping, and also of course how to dissemble, how to keep our thoughts private, how to disguise what we were really thinking or feeling. Most importantly though I think we learned the power of words; how a mean word could hurt and would stay with you for an aeon of guilt, how a kind word had a multiplier effect.

I know that the nuns had hopes that some of us would become nuns in turn. In Grade Five we heard talk of someone in Grade Six who had decided to become a nun. Did that mean she had a calling, or was she the one in her family set aside for religion, or had the nuns seen something special in her — which? It was a bit terrifying, because clearly if you had a calling (the St. Teresa of Avila moment — remember reading her biography during Retreat?), it was almost impossible to resist, and you would spend a lifetime of misery and regret if you dismissed it. I was terrified — I did not want to get that 'calling.' So, in Grade Six I was expecting to have that private chat with the nuns. In my mind it went like this. The nuns (three of them of course): 'Valerie we have followed your years as an Abbey girl, your dedication to studies, your comportment in chapel, your wearing of the Scapular Medal, you being a Child of Mary, and suggest that you are suitable for the Novitiate and a life giving yourself to God.' Me: (shouting internally NO!) 'you are very kind, but my mother would never allow it.' We were all expecting the chat in the last term, about six weeks before final exams. I wasn't called for the chat — I can't tell you the relief, though of course I did wonder (for ten seconds) what this said about me. One of our class did become a nun for a period of time. The underlying assumption was a universal truth: that we would always be Catholic, always be believers, and have 'faith.'

Perhaps the nuns recognized that I knew too well how to dissemble. I think we grasped this concept, without knowing what it was called, by the end of the first year; it was our 'defense against the dark arts.' Do you remember in Grade Four English we had a series of Essays to read among which was one on 'dissembling,' among other concepts? I was shocked and delighted that there was a formal word for what many of us did. It is among the many valuable, unspoken gifts from the nuns: dissembling, independence of thought, challenging authority.

Or the nuns may have remembered my 'rebellion' in Grade One. Do you remember that when we returned after the Christmas holidays they would announce the name of the Class Prefect, having checked our various behaviors over the previous few months? Of course from Grade Two onwards they had decided on Prefects when classes started in autumn. The name of the Grade One Class Prefect was announced with all the solemnity of a papal decree. I know that I hadn't given it any thought; they didn't mention the anointment of Prefects in any of the comics I had read before coming to the Abbey. Yet, I heard 'Valerie Behan has been chosen as Class Prefect.' I have blanked the rest, as I do with most negatives in my life. But about thirty years later I met a sister of Mother Fidelis who said I had caused much amusement later that evening in the nuns' common-room, because I had stood up and said 'Thank you Mother, but I must refuse. I can't take the responsibility.' Well I guess that captures my attitude to responsibility! I expect the nuns saw a very power averse child (I was still only eleven) whom they could manipulate easily. I had no choice really, I was the Class Prefect that year and every year afterwards.

Dear Val,

The thing is, I wanted to be a Prefect. Actually, from the very beginning I wanted to be Head Girl, and saw no reason why I couldn't achieve that title. As for responsibility, I never gave it a thought. I just liked the medal. It was a big thing on a very long chain that you got to wear as Head of Third School (your second year at the Abbey, after wearing a silver Prefect badge for the remainder of the first year). It had the Loreto crest on it, and it was formidable. You were someone when you wore that thing. Symbols must have been important to me. I remember telling Mummy once that I wanted to be a dentist like her and Daddy. She asked why, and I replied that I wanted to wear a white coat! She dismissed me with one of her looks that said volumes as to my rationale for selecting a career. Isn't it ironic that I did indeed get to wear a white coat for most of my academic life.

Sure enough, I was chosen as Prefect that first year when we came back after Christmas. I'm not sure what Prefects did, but I think it had much to do with standing in corridors making sure nobody spoke on their way to chapel, the refectory, games, actually everywhere except the dormitory and when we went to recreation. Do you remember that we had to stop as a nun approached us anywhere in the school, turn, and bow to them as they walked past?

I got used to being a Class Prefect each year and firmly expected to be made Head Girl in my last year. I was so sure, and was totally taken aback when the nuns chose MC instead. It was Mother Consiglio who made the decision. She first appeared when I was in Grade Three or Four, and she and I didn't see eye to eye. It was pretty obvious that I wasn't going to be a pushover; I was far too independent for that. I felt that she got a certain pleasure from thwarting my ambitions. But then again, I was academically at the top of my class, pretty decent at games, not bad at the viola, and definitely going to university. I got to sit at the top table as a run-of-the-mill Prefect in that last year, but that gave me opportunity to express opinions as to how things should be handled — my first foray into Machiavellian behavior that has subsequently proved extremely useful for a life in academia. Years later at a class reunion, one of my classmates insisted that I had been Head Girl. I had to point out that she was wrong, but inwardly I smiled! By the way, nobody *approached me to ask if I would consider being a nun. I suppose that says it all. Still, sometime in my first year at the Abbey I must have got a bit religious, because I remember coming home and insisting that we kneel down and say the Rosary together as a family at home each evening. That didn't last too long, presumably with the lure of playing outside after tea on those long summer evenings. Around that time too I announced to Mummy that I wanted to be a nun. She looked at me neutrally and said: 'You can be a nun if you want, but you are going to university to get a degree first.'*

It's only looking back that I realize how odd a place the convent was. We just accepted the community, which is what they called themselves. But the religious community was as complex as any hierarchical group, with shades of Downton Abbey or Upstairs Downstairs. There were Lay Sisters who did all the cooking, cleaning and laundry. We called them 'Sister,' and knew that they should never be called 'Mother.' But where did we learn that, and how did we distinguish them from the other nuns considering they were all wearing long habits? Most of the Lay Sisters seemed old, but they were genial and kind to us. They died without much fanfare. We noticed because the coffin would lie in their wing of the chapel, not in the nave where the regular nuns had their prie-dieux. Lay Sisters were segregated in the chapel and they even took Communion after the regular nuns. I presume that Lay Sisters had a separate sitting room to the regular nuns, although I think they dined in the same refectory. Did they ever get a day off, a vacation, a change of scenery? Does this sound like slavery?

ABBEY GIRLS

Regular nuns brought a dowry to the convent, or so we understood. We used to speculate as to how much that was, but it was considered an indelicate topic. Often they were university graduates, or were sent to university from the convent. They began as Postulants for a few months, with visible hair and short skirts. After that they became Sisters with no hair showing, a long habit, and a huge Rosary beads hanging from their belt. (Was it the Rosary beads that distinguished them from the Lay Sisters? The beads would not have been conducive to sweeping floors). We knew that regular nuns would take final vows at the end of six years, get a wedding ring as a Bride of Christ, and graduate to being called 'Mother.' Somewhere in that process they symbolically cut off their hair and prostrated themselves on the altar, a particularly fascinating concept to us girls although we never got to see it. As Loreto Abbey was the novitiate for the Loreto Order, most of the new Mothers were sent off to other Loreto convents either in Ireland or abroad, and we didn't see them again. Did they have choices? Did the size of their dowry buy a wider range of career options? Who negotiated the contract? These women were running a huge business with its own version of CFOs, CEOs and COOs, dealing with families, the Church, the State, and also with the governments of third world nations. They were extraordinary, and for some it must have been exhilarating. But for others it must have been grim. Sadly there are few left to ask as to how it really was.

And what drove, inspired or seduced each of them to join the convent? Now there's food for thought. A challenging home environment is the first thing that comes to my older, more cynical mind. But perhaps love of God was the driver in many cases. Still, it would have been a momentous decision in your teens, and once on the bandwagon, it would have been very hard to back out.

Dear Mary

Well that explains the conundrum of the Rosary — you started it! We weren't a particularly religious family. Granted we went to Sunday Mass, we did Lent, the complete Easter Ceremony at the Franciscan or Dominican church, and Confession and Communion as required, but we didn't 'do the Rosary' the way we understood it was done in many households. This would entail the family kneeling together after tea and going through the Ritual. We didn't recite the Rosary at the Abbey, except during Lent, and certainly it was not part of the tradition of either of our parents' families. The Rosary was quite complicated because you had to remember whether it was the turn of The Joyful Mysteries or The Sorrowful Mysteries or another of the five Mysteries. Critically though, they all involved the Decade, i.e., saying the Hail Mary ten times. Any Mystery involved three decades of the Rosary. This was a big commitment from a family, as well as being hard on the knees.

I think it was after the autumn term that you imposed this ritual on us at home. It didn't seem too bad at the time, because the nights were dark, and we recited it in front of the fire in the living room. But I do remember it being short-lived. My heavens, Mummy was so wise, going along with your enthusiasm, knowing that it would be as transitory as the winter season.

Some friends asked me the other day what I did as Class Prefect? Do you know I was a bit thrown, and said 'Oh I just made sure other pupils didn't talk on corridors, that we walked in single file down the stairs on our way to chapel, collected money for various things to speed up purchases at Mother Attracta's emporium, things like that.' Of course they were horrified that we had such silence regulations. But it made me think: what was the function of a Class Prefect?

From the nuns point of view I think I was meant to be a role model of good behavior, helpful to other pupils of whatever age, a volunteer for whatever, and kind and considerate of other girls in the class, and to make sure that class standards (unstated) were upheld. Of course, from my perspective being Class Prefect was a state of being a Loreto girl, as I did not see myself as a natural leader and had no interest in the miniscule amount of power that being Prefect was thought to endow. I remember my anxiety in Grade Two (I was twelve), when the amount of money I had collected for something did not balance the amount I was meant to have. I was so upset, alternately counting my list of payees and the money I had on hand, looking for the missing shillings. We didn't get much pocket money for the term, and making up the missing funds would sop up most of that pocket money. I never thought of talking about the loss with 'the next level up,' Mother Attracta or Mother Fidelis, and asking their advice; I know I would have been too embarrassed to show my lack of accounting skills! Funny, when I think of being Class Prefect that episode comes to mind immediately.

Being Head Girl was different in many ways — making sure that no girls were caught for minor breaking of regulations, and I'm sure I said 'be quiet/don't run, Mother X is just around the next bend in the corridor' millions of times. On the special occasions of High Mass, I and the other Prefects would stand at pivotal points on the corridor to make sure we all went to the chapel in pious silence. And the volunteering could be hilarious; I was a second soprano in the School Choir, a kindness, as I don't even sing along with myself in the car. Mother Philippa was thundering that we were not starting to sing on the beat, and temporarily made me 'lead.' Well we came in on the beat, though I know I was not 'on note.'

My accounting failure makes me think: did we have anyone to ask for advice, or to talk things over with anyone other than our best friends in class? Did we make it up as we went along, or was their some mentoring from older pupils? We certainly couldn't talk to parents about problems; they would have worried and we wouldn't have wanted that. In Grades Four to Six the nuns would invite past pupils to debate with us, talk to us about career choices, and of course we had the sagacity of Mrs. Doran (brought in to advise us on how to be a lady in society), but I'm not sure that we asked for advice much. I know that LR and LM were my rocks. I sat beside LR in Study for the last two years at least, and her comedic sense would get me through anything. Do you remember the Temperance magazine that was part of the allowed reading, in other words, we didn't need to hide it under the covers? It was unadulterated propaganda for foreign missions, and how being temperate (alcohol free) would save us and the children of all nations. Did we ever read it? Maybe once, in desperation during a Retreat. LR latched onto the page where you could sign up for the missions, giving reasons for wanting to 'give your life to God,' and would fill in my details and threaten to give it to her mother to post the next time she came to visit! As I mentioned, her mother helped expose us to contemporary culture each Sunday with the Sunday Times Magazine. I still think of the pleasure of those advertisements with the supermodels of the early 1960s, Jean Shrimpton, and fabulous photographers like David Bailey. LR also had formidable, quiet rebelliousness; she had no interest in sports, as according to her they developed unsightly muscle, and she somehow avoided every hockey game. She just made a point of being so useless at sports that no one, and certainly not Mother Philippa, wanted her on a team. In contrast LM was wonderful at sports. Together, they helped me negotiate school, and being Prefect.

Head Girl had one enormous advantage: I had the trust of the nuns. Do you remember that if Mother Attracta's emporium had the wrong colored threads, or if she had run out of items, we were allowed to walk to Rathfarnham Village to buy this item at the small shop there. It was a wonderful outing on the Saturday afternoons when, for whatever reason, we didn't have home or away games to break the monotony. We would be allowed to walk to the village and back, in couples, in the available one and a half to two hours before afternoon tea. Well, being Head Girl, I could walk to the village by myself. And so the possibilities were endless. The first time I took the 46A bus at the second stop outside the Abbey gates to see how far I could go in forty minutes, I was terrified, madly making up excuses in my head for when I got back to school late for afternoon tea. The bus brought me the whole way to Easons on O'Connell Street in the allotted time. Well now you see the possibilities! During my final year, I took the bus about five or six times and had the chance to read a couple of books completely in Easons in the fifteen to twenty minutes per visit that I allowed myself. I just stood there 'looking through the book' for a longer time than normal. As there were many others doing the same thing, I wasn't noticed. Of course, I was terrified by the possible tap on the shoulder, either in Easons or on the bus, and about arriving back to the Abbey late, but the lure of novels won out.

Dear Val,

As I read your letter, I started to think about money. I don't remember how much we were given each term, but I know it was a precious resource. It was clear that we could not ask for any more unless something fairly catastrophic happened. Nor did we dream of supplementing it with our own savings. They were part of the 'other' life, the one we lived outside the Abbey. Money earned from painting the fence at home in summer (with creosote, if you remember — is it any wonder our immune systems are hardy!), or dusting, or washing the car, was carefully saved for our annual summer holiday driving to the Continent. How did the family car get dirty in the first place? We never ate in it, and Mummy and Daddy weren't the sort to litter. But they smoked, so the windows always needed washing on the inside. And I'm sure that Dad left a trail of mud and oil from his scrap yard trawling all over the floor.

But back to the Abbey. We didn't really need much money, and I don't remember it ever creating a social divide. Instead, table manners and how you said the word 'many' were the real discriminators. Mother Columbanus made sure that we all held our knife and fork the same way with a lecture that first week at school. I remember my surprise that first Sunday. We walked in single file in silence into the gym, herded efficiently by the newly-appointed Prefects eager to show off their skills. Grade One climbed to the top row of the bleachers, with the subsequent classes seated lower down. By this time you were the lone Prefect in Grade Three in Second School, so you would have shepherded your classmates into their rows and sat at the end of them like a full stop. At that time Mother Fidelis was in charge of Third School consisting of Grades One and Two. I don't remember who was in charge of Grades Three and Four, but Mother Columbanus was in charge of the whole school including Grades Five and Six. She was senior to the other two nuns, and glided in last.

She instructed everyone to sit, and we composed ourselves for the Sunday lecture, trying not to fidget, and wondering what she was going to say. She sat in front of us at a small table where a full dinner place-setting had been laid out, complete with real bread, butter and jam. Then she proceeded to show us how to hold a knife and fork. It was wrong to hold the knife like a pen, and she made it clear that we should never again do that. On she went to cutting bread into bite-sized pieces before buttering each of them. Now this was new! Even more intriguing was that you placed a little butter on your plate, and also a little jam — your own private stash for the meal, as opposed to dipping your knife into the shared plates each time you wanted some more. Thinking back, it was quite hygienic: she knew that our knife would be clean at first pass, whereas later in the meal we might have slipped up and licked it! Next came the skill of eating soup correctly although I still don't know why one sips soup from the side of the spoon, and tilts the bowl away from oneself to get the last drops. At any rate, by the end of the hour the whole school knew the right way to do things if you were going to be a lady. This was repeated each year while Mother Columbanus was in charge, and even extended to how to introduce people to one another, the critical issues being age vs. sex vs. religious stature. The gist of this was that the person who hears the others' name first is the winner, in other words, the most important person in the room.

We needed money for sweets which were sold on Saturday morning in the shop run by senior girls. We were limited to spending one shilling and six pence. That probably allowed for one tube of Rolos, a Crunchie bar and a bar of Cadbury's Fruit and Nut chocolate. There were some sweets that were not allowed for whatever reason. I think Tayto Chips were proscribed, so we couldn't wait to go to an away hockey match to sneak into a real shop and buy the banned substance. I suppose we needed money for replacement pens and pencils, although we were all using fountain pens with ink cartridges, not biros. I think copybooks were included in the school fees, and textbooks were definitely covered. If you lost your scissors, or needed more darning wool or a thimble, Mother Attracta took cash. But if for some reason you didn't have enough money, she would write it in her notebook for later payment. It was a small notebook and her handwriting was arthritic and spidery.

Did we use our own money for bus fares to away games? I don't remember. But the other thing I definitely needed money for was raffles. I'm not a gambler, and will happily wander through a Las Vegas casino without dropping a cent. I think I was cured of gambling at the Abbey. Every so often an object would be raffled for the Missions. On one occasion it was a musical box with a ballet dancer who rotated on the top when you wound it up. There was a mirror inside and several little compartments for your treasures. I adored it, and wanted it more than anything else in the world. We were allowed to buy five tickets. Knowing the nuns' mindset, that was probably the equivalent of one week's worth of sweets from the tuck shop. In fairness, there wasn't any pressure to buy tickets, so those who didn't have a spare one-and-six pence, or preferred their sweets, weren't shunned. We hadn't done probability or statistics yet, but I knew the general idea: my chances were very slim. So I made a deal with God. I prayed and prayed and prayed, and promised God that I'd give the jewelry box to Mummy if I won it. I was so certain I was going to win that when the winner was announced in the refectory, I practically stood up before the name came out of Mother Fidelis' mouth. But the name she *called out wasn't Mary Behan. Some totally unworthy girl had got it, and she would likely keep it for herself, not even thinking of giving it to her mother! God took a hit that day, and gambling was axed. I no longer believed in winning by chance.*

TEACHERS

Well Mary,

    I just finished reading John Irving's novel 'In One Person' — what a joy. He describes wonderful teachers, and we had those at the Abbey too. You and I had Mrs. Hogan for English and weren't we lucky because she loved Shakespeare and I think 'got him.' Remember we did a different play each year — starting with 'Julius Caesar,' then 'Hamlet,' 'Macbeth,' 'King Lear' and, my favorite, the 'Merchant of Venice.' I know Mrs. Hogan had to be a feminist as her Portia was strong, not begging, a woman who thought deeply before she spoke. And her Shylock had a reason to be bitter; he was like the Irish with the West Brits looking down on him. Similarly, her Lady Macbeth was someone to be reckoned with, who wrapped those males around her fingers. I don't think she thought much of 'Hamlet' — she always portrayed him as being a bit wimpy.

Though she was a bit torn about the studs, Julius Caesar, Mark Anthony and Brutus, and I think we were similarly torn. I remember that we got to watch the film versions of 'Hamlet,' 'Julius Caesar' (I think the one with Marlon Brando as Mark Anthony), and 'King Lear,' or was it 'Macbeth'? Of course, those have remained my favorite Shakespearean plays, other than 'Henry V.'

Mummy, Mrs. Hogan and Mother Columbanus gave us a love of poetry. We had the Oxford Book of English Verse at home. Do you remember the evocative 'Sands of Dee' by Charles Kinsley? At the Abbey we had the English poetry canon: Wordsworth, Goldsmith, Milton, Shelley, Keats ('Charm'd magic casements, opening on the foam of perilous seas, in faery lands forlorn'), Brontë, Yeats, Swift, Johnson, Tennyson, the Brownings and Gerald Manley Hopkins. We even got a bit of Chaucer and Dante in translation, but of course, given the times, Byron was not on the list.

Mother Columbanus was the ultimate romantic and so she introduced us to the poets associated with the Easter Rising: Pádraig Pearse, Joseph Mary Plunkett and Thomas MacDonagh. I think she dismissed Francis Ledwidge because he was killed in the First World War. And she adored Yeats and anyone who followed him, including Padraic Colum and Austin Clarke. I think Joyce and Beckett were too racy for her, but how she would have loved Seamus Heaney. She was a big fan of Maud Gonne McBride. Many of us would have liked to know more about her life before she entered the convent, and speculated madly; she was such a beautiful woman. And do you remember that wisdom: 'girls if you are out at night try to be in moonlight; fluorescent or sodium lights do nothing for the complexion.'

We had Mother Emmanuel for Irish (Gaelic). She was a relative, perhaps a sister, of Dr. Gogarty the optical specialist in Drogheda. I was okay at Irish, but I did not have the fluency of a Gaelic speaker. I certainly could not have debated or spoke extemporarily in Irish.

And who taught us Science? Ah yes, Mother Carmela. Do you remember it was an agglomeration of Chemistry, Physics and Botany and she was a bit vague. She had no interest in discipline really, and so I'm sure that a lot of girls just skimmed Science. But I loved it. I loved the precision (no hypotheses in Loreto Abbey science). Of course evolution was never mentioned, and Mother Carmela probably only knew Science based on a B.Sc. degree. But she loved plants, and passed on this love to me. Because of her I went to University College Dublin (UCD) knowing I wanted to be a scientist, preferably a botanist. Mark you, after a few Zoology labs at UCD, I really knew what I was going to be.

Did you have the wisdom of Mrs. Doran? Do you remember she was the glamorous mother of girls in grades ahead of me? She was beautifully 'turned out,' something like Mummy, always in the latest impeccable fashion. I mentally checked her out thoroughly because I thought our mother was more glamorous than she. Mrs. Doran gave us the 'grace and charm offensive' course. Of course, that is not what it was called. I think it was called Deportment, but essentially it was about how to dress, make-up, look, behave, and talk to charm, get, and hold the opposite sex. I'm sure she was aware of lesbians, but the force field was directed to snapping up the best of Clongowes, Castleknock, Blackrock and other private boys' schools. I don't remember the details, but certainly impeccable nails, hemline, underwear, frillies, and serene colors were front and center. She talked about color coordination, what to do on our first dates, how to politely refuse, how to attract or really attract a boy, and how to appropriately maintain contact without crossing any 'lines.' And when and how to laugh; she definitely did not condone simpering or weak giggles. We already knew how to deal with cutlery and glasses, though she may have quickly covered that topic again (outside to closest to the plate, unless the hostess has clearly made a mistake). She came in once a month in our final year and imparted Dublin 'class' to us girls from the hinterland. We had Mummy, so already knew most of this, certainly color coordination, which Mummy continued to batter into us for the rest of her life. But, it was wonderful to have a second opinion from another mother.

Dear Val,

Mrs. Doran was the mother of a girl in my class. It must have been weird for the latter to listen to her mother's proselytizing. I remember Mrs. Doran telling us that Friday night should be kept for the '3 Ds'. Needless to say, I've long since forgotten the details of the acronym. But the essence of it was that you washed your hair and body, and one of the 'D's was that you would shave under your arms. This was truly a mystery to me because I couldn't see why. I had nothing to shave. But I thought that the little razors were clever, and I definitely wanted one. Leg hairs weren't included in Mrs. Doran's list, and it wasn't until I emigrated to the United States that I learned about that behavior. You're right though: the object of all of this was to land a nice boy from one of the premier schools who played rugby, marry, have kids, and send them to Loreto convents to perpetuate the tribe. We even had a 'debut' to launch us on the route. Was it the autumn after we left school that we had the Debs dance? Presumably it was organized by the past pupils association, and it was always held in the Gresham Hotel. We had to invite a boy to accompany us, which was considered totally acceptable. It certainly relieved us from the challenge of having a 'fella' in tow so soon after leaving boarding school. We were expected to wear white, and were presented to...to whom? With no Queens or Duchesses in Ireland, who would have been considered social royalty at that time? Mummy brought me to a local seamstress and allowed me to have a dress made exactly to my liking. I found a picture of some glamorous woman in a ball gown in a magazine. Her dress was strapless and seemed to cascade off her chest and back. Even in hindsight, it was a lovely thing. But my breasts were not adequate to support a strapless bra, so I ended up with something akin to a whalebone corset sewn into the dress to support the weight of the fabric flowing down the front and back. I chose a peach-coloured fabric, and was definitely a punctuation mark in that line of white being presented to whomever.

It was Mother Carmela who taught us Science, Botany, Maths, and amazingly enough, Art. We were introduced to Algebra in our second year, and in the beginning I couldn't fathom why the alphabet was being brought into sums. She knew I was bright enough, but that something akin to a revelation was needed before I 'got it.' So she sat down beside me at my desk and gently helped me past the hurdle. The intimacy was overwhelming, and I remember that she smelled 'old'; maybe that's why we never gave her a nickname. After that I loved Algebra, Geometry and eventually Trigonometry. We grew up in the time when girls were not thought to be any good at Maths. All of us took Pass Maths in Leaving Certificate, and rarely did anyone get tutored for the Honours paper. If they were, it was by a teacher brought in especially for the purpose, for none of the nuns were up to it. EH in my class went for the Honours paper, and she was lucky enough to have a man come to the convent to tutor her. We were all very envious.

When I think back, it seems that nobody ever said to us that we couldn't become whatever we wanted. Certainly Mummy and Daddy took for granted that we would pursue whatever career we decided on. But I don't remember the nuns suggesting that some careers were more suited to men than women. It was unusual to have a mother as a dentist; Mummy would have qualified in 1940. She surely would have done something else if her father had not pointed her in that direction. I think she would have enjoyed teaching. And look what she produced: two daughters in academia who spent much of their lives as teachers.

Recently I was chatting to JM and JC who used to

be in my class at the Abbey about the importance of having your own money. I had always thought that it was Mummy who drilled that mantra into us. She used to give us a separate envelope with money in it on our birthdays — separate from the one Daddy gave us, and a lot less. But she'd say: 'that's from me,' and make a point of it. Those Guinness share dividends gave her a measure of self-worth, especially when she couldn't earn a living in Drogheda, as that would have been seen as competing with Daddy and not at all suitable for someone whose husband made a good living. JM and JC reminded me that Mrs. Hogan used to say the same thing to us at school. She would bring newspaper cuttings into English class after the weekend and read out job descriptions for solicitors, doctors, teachers, accountants, and more importantly, the starting salary. Was it any wonder that we assumed we would go to university and have a career that earned a good salary! I don't know if Mrs. Hogan had children, and whether they followed in her footsteps. She was a stern woman, and in hindsight I realize that she must have been in a lot of pain for she had rheumatoid arthritis. Her hands were terribly crippled and she held a book and turned its pages with great difficulty.

Dear Mary,

Well I certainly will never forget your Debs Ball; you were definitely the drama-queen for a few weeks there. I think partly it was that I was in my third year at UCD and having a blast, whereas you were just starting there after the cocoon of Loreto Abbey Rathfarnham, experiencing Lecture Hall A and Professor Carmel

Humphries for the first time. You know, I so envied you that dress; it was glorious. The color especially was gorgeous, that apricot-peach that enhances any pale Irish female. Plus, you were petite, with small hands and feet and it hung on you beautifully. Given my size and broad shoulders, there was no point me trying it on, not that you would have let me!

Mostly though, I envied you your cape. If you remember, what we wore on our shoulders over those dresses was always a conundrum. Mummy did not have a fur shawl or fur stole, whereas every other Mother we knew had several. These were loaned to daughters for the Debs Ball and other parties later in the year. Auntie Mary, who was a genius with a sewing machine, made you a glorious black cape for the occasion. It was luxurious velvet, had a beautiful cowl neck, hung to the top of high-heels and most splendidly, was lined in rich purple silk. Ah, how I envied you Auntie Mary as a Godmother. You may have had your moments with her, but she could sew, and came through with that cape that left mink stoles in the dust. Okay, my Godmother, Auntie Frankie, could knit Irish jumpers brilliantly, but the technical refinement of that cape was beyond her.

I only remember one post-boarding school dress dance because I have a photograph to prove I was there. But I don't think we had a formal Debs Ball for our final year — who knows why? I have no memory of LR or LM in formal gowns. The dress I'm wearing in the picture was lovely; it was cream, but of course, unlike yours, it was far from daring and I have an unexciting shawl around my shoulders. I took Michael, a cousin, as my safe date. Margaret O'Kane is in the picture also, looking lovely, wearing her mother's mink stole, and with David Lyons, who died too young, on her arm.

Hi Mary,

I was talking to a friend about palm trees in Florida and I realised that she did not understand me as I was saying 'palm' with a flat Drogheda accent. Now that is probably why I needed to take elocution lessons at the Abbey while you were spared. I think it may have been Miss Burke who taught us and she was legendary. The first words out of any of our mouths and she could tell us where we were from in Ireland. For those from Cork or Dublin she could tell the street where you grew up. Her task was to give us a hint of the Dublin 4 accent, not too much that we ended up as bland south Dubliners, but definitely enough to get rid of any lingering Drogheda accent. Not all in Grade One had her or probably needed her, but enough of us did that we could trade stories. Those of us that had her attention enjoyed her classes, as we didn't need to study, just to act. She taught us phonetics so that we could understand the difference between 'palm tree' and your 'palm,' and that 'film' was not a two syllable word!

I know that while we were at St. Philomena's in Drogheda we had elocution lessons with Nancy McCarthy, and as a result have all those Speech and Drama Certificates from The Guildhall in London, though I can't remember what we had to do to achieve them. Were these private lessons or was there a group of us? I do remember when Mummy decided my accent needed repair. I had come home from primary school, and regaled Mummy with 'waher,' and 'Saherday' in the flat town accent. She was horrified. Bad enough that our accent was not the sing-song of the West, but I disregarded the presence of a letter 't.' Mummy became friendly with Nancy McCarthy because I think they had similar taste in books, and we visited her for tea at her house at WaterUnder. Do you remember the house? It was rambling, damp, and a stream went by right outside the back door. There was a commode upstairs, but no other indoor toilet. The outhouse though was brilliant, sitting directly on top of that rushing stream. I loved visiting because she was gentle, and always had cake for us.

Dear Val,

Of course I remember Miss McCarthy and elocution lessons because I had a lisp! I dreaded going to lessons with her because I would be forced to stand in front of a mirror and say 'ess' endlessly. I couldn't hear which of my 'esses' was correct, so there was no way that I could activate that dopaminergic reward system in my brain, a neural circuit that was quite well developed already by that early age! My homework for her was to spend hours in front of the huge standing mirror in Mummy and Daddy's bedroom, watching myself as I uttered 'ess' over and over again. Mummy encouraged me, but it seemed futile. Still, as far as I know I don't have a lisp now, so her methods must have worked.

Like you, I remember her house at WaterUnder, a great name for the road on which she lived. It was under the northern end of the Drogheda Viaduct, and you are right, there was always the sound of running water from the stream. Going down her tree-lined driveway felt like entering a watery cavern with the accompanying smell of decayed leaves and humus. She didn't have a car, and bicycled in to town on one of those old-fashioned bikes with a basket up front and a carrier on the back. I remember she was tall, wore glasses, and was a bit intimidating. She must have inherited the house, for there was no sign of a Mr. McCarthy. Going to the upstairs commode was terrifying because you had to take a candle — there wasn't any electricity. Considering I was afraid of the dark, I would pray that I wouldn't have to 'go' when we were visiting her house. The commode itself was a regal affair, quite high off the floor, and when I sat on it my feet didn't reach the pedestal. You are right about the cake though: you could always rely on her for good cakes!

At the end of each year there was a Loreto exam taken by pupils from all of the Loreto schools in Ireland as well as those in Canada, Africa and India.
In her fifth year exam, Valerie got honours in Irish (Gaelic), English, French, Arthmatic, Algebra, Geometry, Latin and Botany. She also came in first place in English among the Loreto students in Ireland.

Merit, Order and Deportment

Dear Val,

When you think about it, the Merit, Order and Deportment thing was a brilliant system. I'm sure it has potential in other places, especially if you eschew capital punishment. It worked for me, although I suspect that other more sophisticated souls in my class ignored it. I didn't want to inquire, as my gullibility would be embarrassing. Think about it: you devise an arbitrary system of 'coinage' and give everyone thirty three of the big ones (Merit), thirty three of the small ones (Order, three of which make up one Merit), and thirty three of small ones of a different color (Deportment) implying that their value is somehow not equal to that of Order, although financially speaking it is.

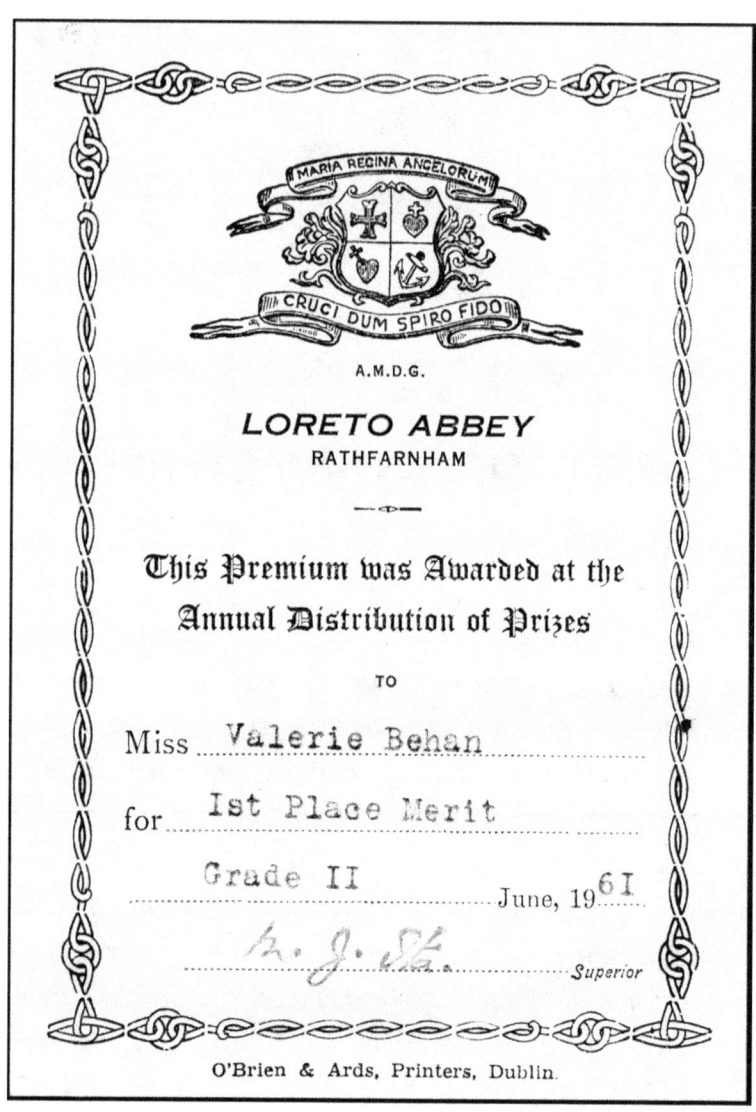

The girl who lost the fewest Merit, Order and Deportment points received a certificate at the annual prize-giving ceremony.

As I write this, it begins to sound like the rules of a new board game, or an early model of the Bitcoin concept. There's a finite period during which the game is played — a term. And in true child-relevant fashion, everyone's a winner except for the few losers, the incorrigibly bold.

The fear of losing a point was with me almost every moment of my six years. It was shame and embarrassment that I feared, although how was anyone to know? And even if they did hear Mother so-and-so announce somberly in the face of a transgression: 'Mary Behan, I am taking an Order point for that,' they were probably far too busy trying to look innocent, or worrying about their own tally to care. The subtleties of which indiscretion deserved what punishment ranked amongst the great legal dilemmas of the time. As I think about it, we never tried to negotiate down either. Surely someone must have tried to plea bargain. But without ever having seen an episode of LA Law, what did we know?

Deportment marks were the most abused. They could be taken for just about anything: a hem too short, an un-darned hole in one's cardigan, running along corridors, coming to chapel without a veil, not bowing to a nun as you passed them. Think about it: their value was equal to Order marks, but they were taken from us with far less thought as to the egregiousness of the offense.

The most amazing thing about this system was its effectiveness. I suppose the final tally was sent home to our parents with each term's Report Card. But what did they know or care? We hadn't burned down the School, been expelled, or incurred serious injury. We were being educated (in Literature, Maths, History and Science, the only items of importance to Mummy), we could hold a knife and fork correctly and we knew lots of Latin hymns.

But back to Game Theory for a moment. The reward's the thing, even if it's subliminal. Well, that's where you have to laugh. The reward was that we got to watch a movie at the end of the term. I don't remember the cut-off, but there were always a few souls who had to stay in Study with a single presiding nun, while the rest of us piled into the bleachers in the gym and allowed ourselves to be transfixed.

There was a precariously balanced screen, clearly an old bed sheet strung between fragile pieces of wood. Facing it was a rented 16-mm projector that inevitably broke the film several times throughout the showing. The film itself came in two or three bulky metal canisters. The whole set-up reeked of 'Cinema Paradiso,' although ours never got that hot in any sense of the word. We used to blame Mother whomever for stopping the reel at certain places (e.g., if there was any kissing). How did she know where to censor? Did she watch it beforehand? And then there were the films themselves. I remember 'The Prisoner of Zenda,' 'Daddy Longlegs,' 'The Three Musketeers,' 'Little Women,' and 'Quo Vadis.' The lights would be switched off, the projector would buzz, and we would sit transfixed in this other world. The sweet shop would have been open earlier in the day (it was usually a Saturday after tea that we got a film), and so we would sit and suck contentedly for the two or three hours involved. I used to pay GM to sit behind me and play with my hair during the show. Now I know that chimpanzees groom each other for free; I had to pay for my grooming with sweets! Finally the lights would come on, and a hundred or more bleary-eyed little girls would leave the gym in single file, across echoing tile floors into that hallway with a low spot in the middle (we called it the Valley), where Sister Mercy had laid out glasses of warm orange juice and Marietta biscuits. And so to bed.

Dear Mary,

    Your letter on Merit, Order and Deportment is the basis for a treatise on our capacity for conformity, especially mine. I can't remember having any worries about losing points, though I must have done so. I think the nuns taught us the rules well in our first term at the Abbey. After that you 'knew' the routine, the areas that were traps for losing Order points because it was easy to be caught 'talking in the corridors,' the losing of Deportment points because of — yea gods, 'running in the corridor.' You learned the senior girls that were lenient when they gave orders, and the ones to avoid, that is, those that enjoyed their power. When you think of it there was no relationship between the nun's Merit, Order and Deportment and the Ten Commandments, so we had two parallel systems to accommodate, the former policed by the nuns and the latter by the priests. I think the priests had a raw deal — how much killing, coveting and adultery could we get up to? We didn't have time to carve graven images, because we were spending too much time making paper roses for the May parade, and we had no choice on honoring the Sabbath. I suppose we could steal. BUT, we had nowhere to hide, and nowhere to hide anything other than in our heads, or perhaps among the junk in our desks. Remember, we had our assigned place in Study for the term and so that small space under the desk lid, with the mélange of schoolbooks and projects we were working on was our security locker. Of course the most inviolate place was our Missals. When you think about it, I mean, if you think about it, we had all those holy pictures: the Pieta, the Holy Spirit, Blessed Virgin, and yes, even St. Theresa of Avila, given us by classmates for birthdays, or winning something, or just because we had finally had a decent dessert. We were meant to have written something inspirational on the back, but in general the message was tame. But no one checked through our Missals, I wonder if any had a love letter or something erotic hidden there — I doubt it.

Did we have films other than for keeping some of our Merit, Order and Deportment points intact? What did the girls do who missed the films? Did we only get to see eighteen films over the six years? I had forgotten about 'The Prisoner of Zenda' — I think we only had it once, but I know we saw 'Jane Eyre' and 'Julius Caesar' and 'Pride and Prejudice' at least twice. In my final year I used to envy the girls who stayed behind in Study. At least they were allowed to read!

Confession

Dear Val,

 I suppose we began going to Confession regularly just before First Holy Communion. We'd have been six or seven years of age. The Catechism was a big deal, and we knew a lot of stuff 'off by heart.' Mummy used to quiz us on it. And like all of our homework, we'd learn it in the kitchen with Alice's help as she ironed sheets in the background, and then present ourselves to Mummy in the living room with 'I've finished my homework.' Whether she believed us or not, she always checked, right down to scrambling the lists of words we had been given to learn to spell. I hated that. I knew them in the sequence I learned them, but she would mix them up and I'd inevitably have to go back to the kitchen to do them again 'properly this time.' Mummy would sit in the living room reading out the Catechism questions and we would recite the answers. Q. Who made the world?

A. God made the world. Q. Who is God? A. God is our Father in Heaven, the Creator and Lord of all things. I know the next question was *'Why did God make the world?'* but for the life of me I cannot remember the answer. It must not have been a good one. We knew the Ten Commandments by heart at an early age, and despite not paying much attention to the list over the years, I can still recite them perfectly. Mind you, *'Thou shalt not covet thy neighbors' wife'* was a bit of a stretch for a seven-year-old girl. And as for *'Thou shalt not commit adultery'* — well, I've no idea how that was reduced to a seven-year-old's level of comprehension. It was pretty clear to me that I didn't have to worry about most of them, but I still would go through the list diligently just to make sure that I hadn't missed anything. No, I didn't kill Mummy this week.

It's really hard to sin when you are a child. The best you can do, especially as a nicely brought up little girl, is to come up with the occasional fib, or a burst of outrage at your big sister with an *'I hate you'* thrown in for good measure. Yet every week we were paraded in single file from St. Philomena's Primary School down Duke Street to St. Peter's church, and lined up in pews to await the priest. He'd appear from the Sacristy with a rustle of garments, an embroidered stole around his neck, and let himself into the confessional. His place in the confessional had a wee gate and a curtain, and sometimes a little flickering red light on top to indicate that he was open for business. On either side there was a cubicle with a full door with a grille in it. I suppose that was to help clear the air in the event of anxious and sweaty penitents. When the person before you came out, you went in and knelt down. The small opening *separating you from the priest was covered by a grille and a sliding door, but if you strained, you could hear mumblings as the person on the opposite side listed their sins. You'd be listening for the telltale sound of the door sliding back, and then a disembodied voice would mumble something through the grille to indicate that you could begin.*

'Bless me Father for I have sinned. It's a week since my last confession.' And it was always a week, except for the times we went on holiday with Mummy and Daddy to Europe where there was no chance of a confession for three whole weeks. I always felt I should have three times the number of sins to declare after those trips, but somehow I didn't. The mathematics of sin counting was not rigorous. But you knew that you had probably told a small lie some time during the week. I suppose that broke the commandment 'Thou shalt not bear false witness against thy neighbor.' It didn't fit into any of the other categories. And of course I didn't do everything Mummy told me or expected me to do, so that was clearly disobedience. I wasn't sure which of the commandments that broke. I suppose it must have been 'Honor thy father and thy mother.' But what if you disobeyed one of the nuns by not staying completely silent in the school corridors? What commandment did that break? Still, it was an easy one to confess, along with hating someone, or being unkind, or being rude to a nun. At the end of the list, I think we must have said 'that's all, Father.' We promised never to do it again and waited for the priest to say something. Most times he didn't, especially when we were so young. So we recited the Act of Contrition, braced ourselves for our penance which was generally an Our Father and a Hail Mary, and escaped from the confessional

with a smug expression of piety. Occasionally the transgressions rose to the level of multiple Our Fathers and Hail Mary's, or even a decade of the Rosary. You always knew who had been bold by how long they lingered in the church after confession saying their penance.

Those poor unfortunate priests. They had to listen to variations on this theme day after day, year in and out, from terrified little girls and boys. I wonder did they laugh and joke about it back in the Priory. I know the confessional is sacred and there's meant to be no telling tales out of it. But our sins were so harmless and must have caused a lot of mirth. Still, the sins and the occasional questions about their details probably said a lot about our home lives, and therefore the lives of their parishioners. How else were priests to stay in touch with the world without something like Facebook? There's probably a conspiracy theory nowadays that confessionals are bugged by the National Security Agency!

I don't think we had those box-like confessionals at the Abbey. In the Sacristy behind the chapel there was a prie-dieu separated from a comfortable chair by a screen, and there Father Sullivan sat and heard our confessions every week. Did we go to confession during Study, or was there some other organization? Regardless, there still was the weekly issue of scouring your conscience for the dregs of sins. I probably told more lies about having sinned than actually doing any sinning. I was hardly going to tell him that I had disobeyed Mother Fidelis' strict instructions not to get out of bed after lights out. One day in my first year, I was dared by some girls in my class to sneak out of bed and get into MC's bed. MC was in on this, fortunately. Of course I accepted the dare, knowing nothing of the hidden meanings associated with this sort of behavior in the nuns' eyes, were I to be caught. I was a complete innocent and didn't know about how men and women got together, let alone women and women. I'd never seen a penis as they were always hidden behind fig leaves, or too small to notice on statues of little boy nymphs and sprites. Sure enough I waited until Mother Fidelis' shadows of undressing were gone as she blew out her candle. The minutes crept by, and eventually I dared to get out of bed, pull aside the curtain quietly and tiptoe several cubicles up the side of the dormitory, counting carefully. It would have been hilarious if I got it wrong. I climbed into MC's bed and froze as Mother Fidelis called out imperiously: 'Is any child out of bed?' There was a breathtaking silence, but Fido was awake! So I had to stay frozen in place with MC for another half an hour until I thought she might have gone to sleep. Unfortunately frozen was not the operative word: MC was plump and warm, and I felt hot and sweaty and...trapped! If I ever had any lesbian curiosity in later years, it was quashed by this memory of female intimacy. I finally got back to my own, safe bed and never left it again for six years.

Dear Mary,

Do you know the Sacrament of Confession has been changed to the Sacrament of Penance — now what daft thinking went into that? I always thought Confession put the emphasis on the really tough part of the process

— having to admit to someone that you had transgressed; the Penance part seemed so much easier. In university I remember going to Confession and admitting to 'sleeping with a boy outside marriage,' an act I had omitted to mention in numerous other visits to the confessional. The admission was the hard part; the penance of three Our Fathers and three Hail Marys hardly seemed justification for the guilt I had harbored for so long!

Looking at it now the Sacrament of Confession is an amazing sociological experiment on the part of the Catholic Church. We are social animals and they gave us the Ten Commandments, which are baseline rules to ensure harmony in society. We started applying them at age seven, ridiculously young in an Ireland of the 1950s, but realistic in a world context. And we had Big Brother, long before NSA or GCHQ, in the guise of the priest who heard our confession. Luckily, he was/is bound by the Silence of the Confessional and so there is no metadata on the malfeasance of us Irish teenagers of the 1950s.

Religion at St. Philomena's firmly ensured that we had good Irish guilt about everything from Christ's Crown of Thorns (we hadn't repented enough) to starvation of the Black Babies (we hadn't given enough money). On top of that, even though we were pre-pubescent, the nuns spent an inordinate amount of time preaching modesty. Mummy sent us to school in shorts one summer for a school outing, and we were sent back home with an admonition that this was immodest clothing. She tried T-shirts, but these were rejected as the V-neck was more than two knuckles from our neck indentation! Long before we knew about breasts or hormones, we had good Catholic guilt.

Religion seemed to become more academic when we went to the Abbey. We moved from the Catechism, our 'little Green Book,' to Religious Knowledge. I think Religion had been removed from the Leaving Cert curriculum at the time, so each school had its own way of dealing with this subject. Loreto Schools did it in style. We had a fairly broad curriculum: it was orderly, we discussed social action, other religions and views of God, and best of all, we competed for the Loreto Medal for Religious Knowledge between schools, as we did for hockey and debating. I won this medal six years in a row. I doubt this says anything about me, other than perseverance and a memory for arcane facts. It does suggest though that Religious Knowledge was not held in as high regard at other Loreto Schools as it was at the Abbey.

We had the Intermediate Certificate in Grade Four and the Leaving Certificate in our final year, but the nuns wanted to be sure we had academic competition in the other years, hence the Loreto Medal. I won this in Grade One, and I was thrilled, but never again; it was short-lived glory.

Dear Val

Reading your last letter made me realize how much we actually learned in those six years. Like you, I won the Loreto Medal one year — Grade Five as I recall. But that exercise of having us compete against all the other Loreto Schools in Ireland in the years when we weren't doing the national exams, was very challenging. You might be top of your class in the Abbey, but where did you stand in relation to other Loreto girls? Intermediate Certificate pitted you against every girl and boy in Ireland of the same age, which put a certain amount of pressure on us. But those results didn't determine your fate. You still had a couple of years to improve so that you could get good marks in Leaving Cert. That exam did determine your fate.

We never thought about co-education because single sex schools were all we knew. I know the debate continues as to whether girls do better in all-girl classrooms. But had boys been part of my every day teenage life, I would definitely have been distracted. Occasionally we would meet someone who was going to a Protestant school, but the notion of boys in the same classroom with us was unfathomable.

In Grade One we had English, Irish, French, Maths, History, Geography and Religious Knowledge. Latin arrived in Grade Two, with Mother Philippa swooshing into the classroom and launching a question before we even began. 'Mary Behan! What is the present pluperfect, third person singular of the verb to run?' I'd practically wet my pants, first with the shock of being put on the spot, then with the mental effort of getting the right answer before she had got as far as the podium, and been obliged to start the class formally with a prayer. Talk about eager; I was like a Border Collie at the Westminister Dog Trials! Of course if you got it right, weeks would elapse before you were asked again. Random trial and reward learning works every time.

By Grade Three we were starting to be 'sorted' into STEM (Science, Technology, Engineering, Mathematics) vs. the Liberal Arts. It's not as if we had to give up the latter; we just added in the former. Well, we did have to give up some subjects, but leaving Art class wasn't a big loss to me. I got a year of German instead which became useful when we travelled to Germany, Austria and Switzerland with Mummy and Daddy in our teens, and I was the only one who knew how to ask for a room. I'm not sure what happened to Geography and History. Did we continue to study them up to the Leaving Certificate? In Geography we learned to draw the outline of every major continent, adding in mountain ranges, rivers, national borders which were fairly stable at that time, and cities. History, rather like human physiology, ended abruptly when things got complicated. We stopped at the War of Independence, the Irish one. After that we couldn't blame the English for winning through treachery, which seemed to be a recurring theme in the previous 800 years. Do you remember that each week we had to write a composition in three different languages: English, Irish and French? No wonder we both enjoy writing. It holds no fear whatsoever. All of our subsequent university exams were also in a 'long answer' format. So I was well-trained to 'Discuss the phylogeny of the Aschelminthes' in a Zoology exam a few years later, writing pages and pages on the topic. I'd love to see some of the exam questions we used to answer, the things I used to know.

Dear Mary

I loved English composition, though I wasn't as enthralled by composition in other languages. It must have been Mother Columbanus or Mrs. Hogan who explained the 'structure' of a composition: first establishing the objective, then bringing together the evidence and finally discussing the whole and bringing it together in a conclusion. At St. Philomena's we had to write compositions such as 'What did you do on your summer holidays?' and I was so abysmal, that I remember Mummy writing most of them for me. The teachers knew of course, even though I adamantly denied her involvement. It was one of my terrors of going to boarding school; how would I do my English homework without Mummy!

Of course once the structure is explained, the rest is easy. And luckily it applies in long-answer exam questions and also in our scientific writings. We were lucky; we could still be floundering like many university students with scads of good results from experiments, but unable to write the Discussion.

I loved Art and was sorry to give it up for the Sciences, but Mummy had already decided that I didn't have talent. Best of all, I could draw and paint left-handed and my left-handedness was accepted. I had been forced to write with my right hand at St. Philomena's, enforced by a cloth binding my left hand. Do you remember that Mummy had a policy of no complaining about school, so I had not told her about my hand being bound. Eventually I told her and she was furious, and told the nuns to stop the practice. But the change-over was in the process, the nuns continued, and I ended up writing with my right hand but still sewing and drawing with my left hand. At the Abbey the nuns were more enlightened; they were mainly interested in the end product.

I still have my Leaving Certificate showing that I ended with honours in Irish, English, Latin, French, Physics and Chemistry and Botany, and with Pass in Maths. The latter is the thing I regret; it would have been so much easier to do Honours Maths at the Abbey, where the nuns would have brought in a decent teacher, than at UCD. Maths during First Year in UCD was one of the Sacred Mysteries. We had that awful lecturer, who spoke to the chalkboard in a whisper. As a result, all except the ex-Christian Brothers pupils needed evening tutorials (grinds) to hope to understand calculus. My Intermediate Certificate shows Honours in all the above and History and Geography, so I must have done those subjects until Grade Four. I'm looking through the Loreto Exam certificates and have just read that in Grade Five, I came first in Ireland in English. I never noticed before, I think because the writing is in Mother Columbanus' memorable script — a work of art rather than information.

Retreats

Dear Mary,

    Can you imagine Retreats in this social networking age — the idea of keeping silent for three days and nights? I can't remember whether we looked forward to Retreats as a break from classes and study, or whether we dreaded the enforced silence. Of course, we could have avoided complete silence by passing notes, but I remember us being remarkably compliant during Retreats. In post-Loreto years two classmates recounted how both of them went separately (but at the same time) to the farm adjacent to the Abbey during our breaks from chapel. They were meant to be reading holy texts, but instead went riding horses bareback in a field. They broke all kinds of rules by leaving the Abbey grounds, much less trespassing on the farmer's property. But they never spoke to each other and so didn't break the cardinal rule: silence.

When you think of it, those lectures from the priests were such a bore. Do you remember, each year we had a different Order of priests in to talk to all of us three times a day in the chapel. And this on top of Mass and confession! We would have priests, essentially young lads in their thirties, railing on about the life of Christ, penitence, Hell, a life of chastity and denial. Being a bit cynical, you had to think they were talking about and to themselves. You probably don't remember the year we had a very strict, almost hermetic order running the Retreat. They were particularly vocal on chastity and self-denial and avoiding 'temptations.' Of course the words 'sex' and 'boys' were never used. In retrospect it is funny — lectures on temptation, without explanation. You'll remember we had to go to confession with these priests, and I remember the one I went to implying that I must touch myself. Now, I was definitely pre-puberty, or at least pre-knowledge of sex, so the confessional interaction was as though we were speaking different languages. I was used to our usual once a week confession, where the worst 'sin' was being mean to someone. But this priest questioned me on whether I touched myself 'with my hands' when I had a bath. My reply was 'Well no father, I use a face-cloth.' Yea heavens, I was innocent! Then he questioned me on whether I touched myself 'down there.' Again, incomprehension from me. I thought he couldn't hear well and repeated the bit about the face-cloth. He said 'Well I'm sure you do' (touch yourself down there) and I realized he wasn't deaf, and there was an innuendo here, though I had no clue what it was. After a few more tries on his part, I think I might have agreed that I touched my toes with my bare fingers, and I was let go. I was annoyed at myself because I couldn't get him to understand (and he was only from the Midlands, not incomprehensible Kerry), but I realized that there was something wrong because some of the older girls were crying as they left the confessional.

The silence, and walking the grounds reading spiritual texts are the best memories I have of Retreats. We had no classes, no studying and no 'rounds' (running three times around the grounds regardless of the weather — a mile at least). I think the food was better also. Of course what we read was meant to be uplifting, such as the life of St. Teresa of Avila, or some other saintly and well-educated woman, or the life of Father Damien as he ministered to the lepers in Molokai. But I think most of us had novels hidden inside the religious covers, otherwise how could we have stood it? I know that Teresa of Avila's life put me in the 'fear of God' of ever being 'called by God' or experiencing a vision — and of course Mummy would have been horrified. Do you remember how little patience she had for the religious thing? I think I wanted to be a nun sometime in my eleventh year, and she said 'Yes Valerie, but not until you are thirty' (can't you hear that voice?).

But you know, I'm so glad we went to a school that had Retreats — they have proved their worth. They were preparation for long periods that we have spent without human company: driving across Canada and the USA for work.

ABBEY GIRLS

Dear Val,

The parallels and differences between our two sets of experiences are fascinating. About the same age as you, I came home for the holidays and told Mummy I wanted to be a nun. Needless to say, she knew that time and my predilection for boys would cure me of that temptation.

Retreats — they were wonderful! They happened in spring, maybe April, and it was glorious to be able to walk around the grounds with no agenda. We didn't have to do 'rounds' after breakfast, or play hockey. And we didn't get visitors during those days, so no parading parents around like prisoners in a penitentiary. All in all, it was a marvelous three days. I do remember the very strict priest who came and pontificated fire and brimstone. But I was much younger than you, and didn't have much of a frame of reference. We certainly looked forward to having a Retreat priest after months of Father Sullivan and the pimply altar boys. And as for touching myself, well, here's my story.

You must have been at university when we had a youngish, Dublin-sounding priest. I don't know what religious order he was with, but I often think back on him and how sensible he was. Remember, we were allowed to visit the priest in the priest's parlour for a private conversation, aside from confession, if we wished. Well, I had a question and he seemed like the sort who might be willing to give me a truthful answer. A few years earlier I had asked Mother Francis what was circumcision. She taught us Religious Knowledge and had a very large bosom. We used to joke that she could support the text book, open, on her starched white bib! I had probably read the word 'circumcision' in the Bible, which we were allowed to read in the chapel. It would have been a difficult book to ban, although I don't think that the nuns liked the idea of us reading the Old Testament. At any rate, I asked the question of Mother Francis during Religious Knowledge class, and her response was: 'they say prayers and sprinkle Holy Water.' I can just see the look on a Rabbi's face! In retrospect though, it was a wonderful answer, because she probably didn't know the details of circumcision either.

So my question for the priest was: 'what is masturbation and can girls do it?' Now, when I went into the priest's parlour, he offered me tea or a sherry. It struck me that for the first time ever at the Abbey, I was being treated as an adult. So I behaved as one, and declined graciously (we were nothing if not gracious to priests). He then went on to explain. First he went through boys, a penis and masturbation. I feigned knowledge, never having seen a penis. If you remember, our Physiology textbooks at boarding school had been surgically altered to remove the chapters on reproduction. We learned about heart, lungs, even kidneys...but those ureters just went nowhere! So as far as we knew, there was nothing below the kidneys. Fortunately, you had shown me your Zoology notes from first year at university, which had a diagram of the reproductive system of a dog. So I had some idea of how boys worked. With the aid of a textbook and diagrams, he pointed out what I had: a labia majora, a labia minora, and a clitoris. Then he said that the next time I took a bath, to touch myself there, but not to prolong it. It was spoken in such a matter-of-a-fact way that that's precisely what I did. It felt vaguely strange and nice, and like a good girl, I moved on to the business of washing before the five inches of hot water we got in the bath grew cold. I sometimes wonder what it must have been like for a young priest to be sent to us for a Retreat. Did they like it? Were they terrified at the prospect of listening to 150 girls' confessions? What possessed this fellow to bring along a textbook on reproduction? And what were the other books he brought?

By the way, my cachet rose considerably after you gave me your university Zoology notes. Although the diagrams were of a dog's reproductive system, I could knowledgeably say that testicles had to hang down because sperm needed a cold temperature. I was like the Oracle of Delphi to my class that term!

Rituals and Traditions

Dear Mary,

Thanks a million for sending me the book on Loreto Abbey that past pupils got at the final school reunion in 1999; it triggered so many memories of rituals and traditions. Traditions were the precious and wonderful punctuations to the school year. In Grade One we didn't know what to expect. Each day we were learning the rituals of boarding school life, so diametrically different from what we might have anticipated from comics. Is there any way comics could have prepared us for daily Mass or for the morning 'rounds,' where the only surprise was whether we ran clockwise or counter-clockwise?

We were slowly introduced to traditions and I suppose we didn't recognize their importance until our second year. There was a High Mass close to Christmas for which we practiced singing for weeks in the autumn term. We practiced for aeons and only sang any particular Mass once in our six years at the Abbey. I listen to Gregorian Chant occasionally to try and capture the feeling. Honestly, you could feel like 'giving yourself to God' if all that involved was continuous Gregorian Chant. Maybe it was our glorious chapel that made the sound so resonant. Did you know it was built in 1840, and Augustus Pugin was the architect. He's famous for his work in Gothic Revival architecture, and worked on St. Barnabas' Cathedral, Nottingham and the interior of the Houses of Parliament in London. The chapel had such a calm, graceful interior and wonderful acoustics; sound rose and reverberated and the final sung Mass was always better than when we practiced in the gym.

I know that the annual Play was a tradition, and I really loved it, but I always had a minor role, and certainly never spoke, and so it was a yearly event that I didn't anticipate wildly. Rehearsals were deadly. I mean you only need to learn once where you were to 'enter stage' or 'stand on stage.' And then we hung around while those with talking parts practiced. Though I'm really glad of what I picked up along the way at those rehearsals. I can't act, but I do know how to project my voice, make eye contact with the masses, and deliver, thanks to all that standing around at rehearsals!

It was the annual Picnic that was the most pleasurable unexpected tradition in Grade One and all the years after.

The annual picnic was an opportunity to push up our divided skirts. Mary is second from the left.

We didn't have to do anything other than pray for good weather on the appointed day, but I think the nuns were flexible, because the weather was always glorious. We piled onto carts, drawn by the farmer's horse or tractor and went to the fields above the Abbey in the grounds of the Priory. This was another grand estate, and if you remember it was opposite St. Enda's where Pádraig Pearse had lived. The Priory itself was associated with Robert Emmet. As these two were pivotal in Ireland's fight against the British, Pearse with the Easter Rising and Emmet with the Rebellion, they were two of our martyrs, our Che Guevaras. The Picnic gave Mother Columbanus an opportunity to repeat the history of the Easter Rising which has to be part of our Irish DNA in any case. We didn't go far, I remember the whole journey to be about twenty minutes, but we were away from school in the fields looking down on Rathfarnham and Dublin. We were in the Dublin Mountains, and could loll about on the grass, and not have to do anything for a whole afternoon. The nuns piled the carts with lemonade and biscuits and we could hedonistically eat junk for an afternoon. You know the Picnic is a memory of Loreto that many past pupils mention in the book that you sent. I think its because at the Picnic we were free from the obligations and everyday rituals of school.

Now a tradition that I got to experience, but you missed, was the hundred-year anniversary of the death of Mother Theresa Ball, the nun who founded Loreto Abbey Rathfarnham. She died in 1861, hence the centenary. This Anniversary was a big deal for all of us. The Mother General of the Loreto Order, who in my mind was at the right hand of, and superior to the Pope, was coming for the event. The Pope was John XXIII at the time, and he looked like a benign Mafia Don. We knew the name of the Pope, but none of us knew anything about Mother General or her provenance. Were all Mother Generals Irish in the same way all Popes were Italian? She was visiting the Mother House for the Mother Teresa Ball Anniversary and the place was cleaned to an inch of its life. More importantly though, we pupils would honor the Mother General and the occasion by a North Korean-style human formation on the front lawn. We were all dressed in white pinafores and wore our white veils, and the idea was that we would be arranged like the Loreto crest on the lawn. Mother Philippa had to be behind this idea don't you think? I'm not sure whether we ever achieved Kim Jong-Il style harmony, but we did kneel low and bow in some kind of formation. The only picture from the event has us in Napoleonic squares. I don't remember much else, but I'm sure we must have had about three masses that day.

Well, the Japanese beetles have been demolishing my single, hardy rose bush and their parasite — a Tachinid fly I've been told, has not come to this region of Canada as yet, so I'm thinking of getting rid of the rose bush. But how could I get rid of something that reminds me of May at the Abbey, another wonderful tradition.

Do you remember that May was dedicated to Mary the Blessed Virgin and we celebrated her in style? I'm not sure when we began making the artificial roses, but we had to produce millions. I think we were introduced to the practice soon after returning from Christmas holidays.

A class was issued with rolls of crepe paper in various shades of red and off-red. The rolls would be cut into around two-inch slices and each of us would cut petal shapes with scissors and then shape and mold our roses. We tied the bottom with green ties and loosely piled the finished product into cardboard boxes. Of course, today there are multiple You Tube videos showing how to make the roses, and even better, crepe comes in ribbons of various widths. But, as Abbey girls we learned this talent with only a Novice showing the way, though there may have been some with adventurous mothers who had already introduced this 'talent.' I'm not sure that anyone got out of rose-making duty; you would need to be particularly inept to fail at this task, though I think LR, who sat at the desk to my right in Study, made roses that looked like miniature bombs. For weeks afterwards we would find bits of crepe paper in corners of our desks, or corners of the Study. Making these roses squashed any later urge for home-made crafts. Just as well, Mummy would have hated the untidiness — she only tolerated us crafting doilies!

The artificial roses were backups, just in case the rose bushes in the Abbey gardens were late, or the weather was too awful to collect petals. But you know, I don't remember ever using the artificial roses, do you? Perhaps the artificial roses were a kindergarden plot to keep us occupied on winter days when we couldn't go outside at recess. Though, as I remember doing 'rounds' in snow, I don't think that was likely.

Whenever we celebrated May Day the weather was always glorious. The paths where the priest (in his best chasuble and swinging the thurible) and the acolytes would walk were covered with rose petals in all the wondrous colors that roses in Ireland can produce. Who got the petals ready? It certainly wasn't us. I think they must have sent all the Postulants and Novices out the evening before to prepare this visual feast. We followed the priest in a regimented order. I don't remember what that was, but probably behind the Novices. I must have been ahead of you, though.

Dear Val,

When I think of traditions, it's Prize Giving that comes to mind (although the Picnics were great). I was such a competitive thing. Give me a race, any race, and I would strive like an Olympic athlete. And like Gollum with the Ring, I coveted medals. You came home from your first year with a fabulous hunk of silver — the Religious Knowledge medal. I was SO impressed. There and then I decided that I would get one of those, and I did succeed in my first year, but never again. You, on the other hand, came home for six years in a row with an increasingly beautiful medal, the ultimate being a hunk of gold in Grade Six. The Religious Knowledge exam was a very formal affair, held in the gym where we sat at individual desks, so far apart that there was no chance of cheating, although it would never have crossed our minds being Loreto girls. The exam was set by the nuns for all Loreto Schools in Ireland, and likely for schools in India and Mauritius too. I don't know if I told you, but I met a girl at the university here who went to Loreto in India, and as we compared experiences, I realized that you could have substituted the Abbey for Calcutta, with the only difference being that they were warm! I studied hard for those Religious Knowledge exams. So I was shocked every year at Prize Giving to discover that I hadn't won the medal. In fairness, as I was at the top of my class in every other subject, it wasn't unreasonable to think that I would get the religious medal. Year by year I continued to try to ace that exam. But for whatever reason (maybe I wasn't really religious!), I failed. So at Prize Giving I would get called out to come up to the podium in the Concert Hall to accept my other prize, but never the one I really wanted.

For the first few years the prizes for coming first in your class in academics were pretty good. I don't remember exactly what they were, but it seemed worth the effort. Probably a photo album with an embossed leather cover, or an 'object' that you and your friends could admire in your cell for the next few years. Then one year, as a prize (Mother Consiglio must have been responsible for this), I was handed a biography of Joan Sutherland. I was stunned. First of all, I hadn't a clue who she was. But when I eventually read the 'blurb' telling me that she was an Australian soprano (and rather like you, I couldn't sing a note), I realized that I was never going to read it, that nobody would admire it, and that the whole year of studying was for naught. Fortunately my competitive juices kicked back in the next year on schedule...still hoping for that Religious Medal.

Games

Dear Val,

Saturdays were special. First of all we didn't have to get up so early — Mass was at 7:30. The day loomed ahead with endless treats: no classes, sweetshop, reading, games. Did we still have Study on Saturday evening? I know that recreation was an hour instead of the usual half hour. After breakfast we went back to our dormitories for something, the actual name of which escapes me. But it involved Novices and Postulants who were dispatched to check our personal hygiene, laundry, and anything else that came up. I suppose it was an effort on the part of the nuns to check on our welfare, using the Novices as a go-between. They didn't ooze discipline, chatted to us about all sorts of things, answered questions that we were afraid to ask the nuns, and all the while kept an eye out for deviant behavior, I suppose. We had toothcombs, and I adored having my

ABBEY GIRLS

hair combed through (in search of lice no doubt). It was like a head massage because I had really fine hair that didn't snag. Most of the girls hated it because of the comb snagging on their luxurious, long, or curly hair, something I yearned for. The Novices would go through our lockers to make sure we had folded our clothes, changed our underwear, and mended and darned socks and cardigan elbows. How many pairs of underwear did we have, or socks? I think we changed once or twice a week, at most. We must have ponged. Certainly we had one plaid shirt for the weekdays and a white one for Sunday. Socks, undies, shirts, towels and washcloths were put into personal laundry bags and dispatched into huge hampers at the end of the dormitory. That lot had to be lugged down three of four flights of stairs by the Lay Sisters to an annex that probably resembled the Magdalen Laundries, had I known about them at the time. By the time the Novices and Postulants were finished with us, the sweetshop was open. That too was restricted. You could spend one shilling and six pence (when you think of it, a lordly $1.50 today), and the senior girls took it seriously to ration your intake. Of course you could trade. Mother Attracta's emporium was open on Saturday mornings too, for thread, needles, nylon stockings, suspender belts, sanitary towels, soap and toothpaste.

If you were going to an away hockey game, you had an early lunch where Sister Colette, the nicest of the Lay Sisters, gave you freshly cooked food, not the usual stuff that had sat around in warming ovens for an extra hour or two. At most meals, vegetables weren't so much cooked as destroyed by putting them on to boil at the same time as the beef or mutton roasts went into the oven after breakfast in the morning.

For games, we had divided skirts that had to reach the ground when you knelt. There were some risqué girls who managed to take theirs up an inch or two, especially as they would be on display in Dublin City, and potentially visible to boys. We'd strap our hockey boots to the end of a hockey stick, don a winter coat or a blue blazer (complete with crest), and head off to catch the 46A bus in Rathfarnham Village. If you weren't going to an away game, it didn't matter. Everyone was involved in hockey games, no matter how useless or reluctant an athlete. The visiting teams would arrive in the early afternoon, and Mother Philippa or another athletic Novice would get the game going. Hockey was a big deal, with the Loreto Shield as the visible prize, sitting proudly in the visitor's hall for a year when the Abbey won it. There were try-outs each year, and you'd be assigned a team with little chance of moving up unless you did something remarkable on the hockey pitch that was seen by Mother Philippa or the Games Captain. We worshipped the Games Captain. She was always beautiful (AB is one I remember in particular), tall and slender, and SO good on a hockey pitch, gliding effortlessly from center to goal. She was usually a Prefect too, and sat at the coveted head table in the refectory. If you hosted a visiting team, you got to share tea and biscuits with them before sending them back to Bray or Foxrock, or St. Stephen's Green or Balbriggan. The rest of us went to the refectory for the usual bread and butter, fruit and tea.

Hockey games were played against teams from other Loreto schools around Dublin. Mary (front row, left) played on the winning Seconds team in Grade Six.

Then you could read and loiter until the away teams came back with tales of victory or defeat. The rest of Saturday becomes vague. We wrote letters, read, went to chapel for prayers, and had tea in the evening. I think we got something special for tea on Saturday. I have this image of us dancing with each other (waltzes, of course) at recreation, because all the classes were in the gym together that evening. This was different from recreation on week days, when Third School, Second School and First School had the gym separately. Too much mixing of classes was not encouraged as I expect the nuns thought it would lead to unhealthy crushes. And then to bed where there would be muffled sounds of crunching on a last bit of Kitkat, or some other sweet treat that had been smuggled into the dormitory.

Well Mary,

We have not talked about laundry because I think that is where we may have the most divergent memories of the Abbey. We had our nametags sewn into every piece of linen, and outer and inner garments that we owned. Other than stockings, which were subject to ladders and so needed replacement during the school year, nothing darkened the door of the Abbey without a tag. It was the nun's NSA system, a misplaced garment was easily tracked — did we lose anything? I can't remember how we decided what items needed to go to the laundry. Was it an automatic 'once a week for undergarments' deal? I think so, because I know that I'm a dab hand at washing just the armpit and crotch areas of clothes, and that would have been essential as we had no access to deodorant.

I can't remember the process of sending clothes to the laundry, but I do remember the return on laundry day. There were those vast baskets of clean laundry that arrived in each dormitory, or in the case of when we were in rooms, arrived on each landing. I remember that the laundry was higgledy-piggledy, and our job was to get our name-tagged items home to our bed where we could fold them and store them in a way acceptable to the controlling Novices. In my memory, we dived in and hauled out an armful of mixed items — socks, vests, handkerchiefs, towels, and then went running around the dormitory, bestowing items on the owner's beds; one sock for MB, a towel for AB, another sock for AC, and then at the bottom of the load, the second sock for MB! I remember it as a joyous free-for-all.

I loved games, but have no clue how we were any good at them. We really had no training at St. Philomena's in Drogheda, where I remember the most challenging games to be marbles and conkers. I think a bit of Dad's athleticism must have rubbed off on us, and we used to play tennis with the O'Kanes. Ah yes, we played croquet too. I know I gave up golf at an early age. You remember that we had lessons at Baltray Golf Club and we were meant to practice. I would beg you to play with me, because you could see where I hit the ball (I didn't know I needed glasses at that time) and you would bellow out 'Fore!' without embarrassment. I could hit the ball straight, but the question was — straight to where?

Somehow at Loreto Abbey all the limb and hand-eye coordination came together, and we could play hockey, netball and tennis and were good enough to make teams. I played defense for a while and also right wing. Now that's a magical feeling — running down the pitch, the head of the hockey stick hovering above the ground, and catching and running with a pass, and then in turn making a smooth pass to the centre-forward ending in a goal. I wasn't much use at scoring goals, but I could pass cleanly.

We put so much into games, but I'm sure the nuns saw this as a way to keep 'bad thoughts' and hormones at bay. We had the half-hour for 'rounds' in the morning, running around the grounds three times, passing the statues, the walled garden, going by the wood and the pond no matter what the weather. I think we even did rounds in snow. Hard to avoid those, though LR did, claiming weak Achilles, or mediolateral calf muscle spasms, or whatever. And then there was more practice after dinner in the middle of the day. Ah, now I remember how we got hooked: it was the Loreto approach to group envy that predated Mark Zuckerberg by years. We arrived as new pupils in September. After dinner the first full day we went out into the grounds knowing nobody. But there in front of us were the two hockey pitches with teams of older girls wearing hockey boots and carrying hockey sticks, running around, practicing, laughing and joshing with their friends! Of course we wanted to be them, and could be, IF we lived up to Mother Philippa's criteria and showed some talent at 'try-outs.'

Even though LR disparaged the whole process and

I think avoided being on any team during six years at the Abbey, I loved team sports. We had the home and away games on Saturday afternoon and the tea and biscuits associated with those. Best of all were 'away' games to distant Loreto Schools, especially Foxrock, Dalkey and Balbriggan which required at least two bus rides and maybe a train to get to them. I think the nuns had worked out exactly the connections we should take, so there was little flexibility for hopping into a sweet shop except on the Foxrock and Balbriggan 'aways.' On the train ride to Balbriggan, I used to fantasize that the train would forget the Balbriggan stop and continue on to Drogheda, where Mummy and Dad would be waiting for me at the station, of course.

I think all Loreto Schools in Dublin bought from the same supplier, because the biscuits and tea after the game were the same in all, except for Loreto St. Stephen's Green, where biscuits were better. Unfortunately, those girls weren't all that good at games, and tended to be knocked out of the running early, so we rarely had the treat of their biscuits.

Ah, the joy when we missed a bus somewhere in the city and had to wait for the next one — twenty minutes of freedom. I don't think we were allowed to go into shops (we were only interested in sweet shops), but would do so, a few girls at a time, so we would not be too conspicuous.

Anne was here for the weekend and we got talking (somehow) about Title IX that came into law in the USA in 1972, the year she was going to high school. She said a big difference between the school experience that she had by comparison with her elder sisters was because of Title IX; she was involved in competitive, intramural sports, and they were not.

Well that gave me pause, and made me realize how lucky we were at Loreto Abbey in ways I hadn't thought of when we were there. We took for granted, at least after the shock of the first term, that we would be involved on some sports team and that, if we were good enough, we would compete with other Loreto Schools. Prior to talking with Anne, I never realized how privileged we were. And competition was not just confined to other boarding schools. We competed with Beaufort (a day school close-by), The Green (day school), Foxrock (was it day or boarding?), Dalkey (again, day or boarding?) and Balbriggan and Bray (had to be boarding). So we were a group of seven Loreto Schools who competed for various Loreto trophies. And we had a number of sports — I think we competed intramurally at hockey, netball, tennis and debating.

Being boarders we had no 'helicopter parents' driving us to sport events. The nuns were not free to leave the convent and so we had the luxury and extraordinary freedom of going with a responsible senior girl. And of course, sports teams had participants from different classes. I just checked a photo of one sports team and there's myself and JM, who was two academic years below me. The conversation with Anne also had me thinking of how we were saved from helicopter parents, in a sense from any parents, except at holiday times. While we were in school, our parents had three essential functions: visit on a regular basis, bring something interesting to eat, and write us a letter, so that we would feel special (occasionally) when letters were handed out in the refectory. We were spared from any conflict about bedtime, doing homework, being clean, what we were reading etc., and from any mother-daughter hormonal conflicts. When you think of it, even the Dublin girls who usually came as boarders in the last two or three years of school, could only see their parents on a Sunday. What a shock it must have been for them, being part of a tightly knit family unit as day pupils until they were thirteen or fourteen, and then being sent to boarding school when puberty really hit.

School holidays were a disjunct phenomenon — we were 'away at school' and then 'at home.' School friends did not crossover into friends at home, as they were usually from very different parts of Ireland. We returned after two months of summer holidays and picked up with friends as though holidays had not intervened. I don't think I ever spoke about holidays with school friends — they were independent events, and I'm sure this helped us when we emigrated to North America. Many of our friends in Drogheda were also boarders, just not at Loreto Abbey. I don't think I ever considered that pupils at Beaufort, which when you think of it was just across the road from the Abbey, had a daily home life. I pitied them because they had to do Home Economics, with the only product seeming to be elaborately iced cakes. I never thought of them having 'parental conflict,' possibly on a daily basis. Our lives were compartmentalized on a semester basis.

*Valerie was captain of the winning
Firsts team in Grade Five.*

THE PARLOUR

Dear Mary,

    I don't remember visitors as much as I remember the PARLOUR — I think that word deserves capitals — it was such an important room. First of all it had that real Downton Abbey look about it. I've been in other rooms like that, visiting the Coddington's at Oldbridge House with Dad — all those West Brit accents, or the lounge in some very large, old Irish hotel. But the Parlour was unique. In retrospect, it was a room that needed a large fire going constantly to give it a human touch, but of course there was never a fire. Not that we would have noticed; we were just there for Visitors. Do you remember every Sunday at dinner in the refectory just hoping like anything to be 'called to the Parlour' between 1:00 and 3:00. Mummy and Dad came on a fortnightly basis (one or other of them — rarely together), so we knew their routine, but I was always hopeful for a relative to turn up out of the blue, who would rescue me from my envy of the lucky others. Do you remember Barry McHugh coming to visit us with Irene when they got engaged? He is always on my personal Olympic pedestal list because of that. I have no clue who he was trying to impress by the visit (we were too insignificant to count) but he visited and walked the grounds with us and we got to show off a presentable cousin and his glamorous fiancée.

Do you remember we would tentatively open the Parlour door and look around for 'our' Visitor(s)? Chairs were clustered in groups at the various extremities of the room, and there would be Mummy or Daddy waiting for us. If the day was wet, we groups of pupils and visitors stayed in the Parlour and tried to keep our voices low so as not to disturb the other clusters. We didn't have the option of suggesting a walk to the dormitory or gym, though maybe we could have brought visitors to the chapel. Which makes me wonder — did our parents ever get a tour of the school before we went there. I doubt it. Rather, I think they were interviewed as to our suitability for being Abbey Girls and, with our acceptance as pupils, should just consider themselves as among the chosen.

If the weather was good we could walk the grounds. Now that was wonderful. We would go down the central walk, by the big chestnut trees and usually turned left at the end, on the way to the orchard and walled garden, and then back by the pond with the swans. We might have got two rounds out of Mummy, but by then she would be bored, and would start mentioning the long drive home and having to get 'Daddy's tea.' Daddy, on the other hand, would walk around as long as we wanted, but we never really had more than one to one and a half hours for Parlour. Who else visited? In theory, boys wouldn't, as they would be daunted by the frozen glare of the nun on sentry duty at the large entry doors. But Aiden and Fergal, Daddy's friends from Dundalk, then at UCD, braved these stares in my sixth year. They absolutely charmed Sister at the door, explained how they had been asked by Dad (putatively sick) to visit us, and how they had gone out of their way to do so. Neither was remotely interested in either of us; like most of Dad's younger friends, we were 'the girls' to them. However, they were interested in assessing the 'talent' in sixth year — girls possibly going to university the following year. They insisted on walks up and down the central walk (no turning left for them), checking out girls playing hockey, etc.

I so envied girls called to the Parlour every Sunday. Did they know how extraordinarily lucky they were? And then we ached for all the pupils whose parents, relatives and friends were far away, or in other countries (England, Lebanon, Spain, India in my years) who were never called. How did they stand the loneliness? I know that I would hope so much for a visitor and then when no one materialized, I would go and sit on the toilet (I forgot, this was another place we could hide, at least for five to ten minutes) and think 'this is a dream, I'm going to wake up and I'll be at home.'

Of course, being called to the Parlour at any time other than a Sunday might not be good news. When this happened, we might not see the pupil for the rest of the term. But I had a positive 'call' in first year that I don't think I told you about. It was to read a poem. I was told that there was going to be some film made and they wanted the voice of a young girl reciting the poem 'Great wide beautiful wonderful world' by William Brighty Rands. I think it was just the first verse of the poem:

> Great, wide, beautiful, wonderful World,
> With the wonderful water round you curled,
> And the wonderful grass upon your breast
> World, you are beautifully drest.

The nuns had chosen me for the recitation, and I read the verse a few times and then spoke it about three times into a microphone. I was told not to talk to others about this, and that was that. A few weeks later I was called to the Parlour again and told that another young voice was chosen and I got a box of chocolates! I had something to share with others so I was happy, and of course, will never forget that verse.

I think there was a bookcase in the Parlour also — am I right? It was under lock and key, but if we were good we could borrow books from it. And so began my reading adventures into the appallingly written lives of various saints and the much better written adventures of the Jesuits in North America. Although these books were riddled with prejudice and anti-Indian sentiments. Now why didn't we have a decent library — that's what I've wondered since being at the Abbey — it was pathetic, and what did the nuns read? We gobbled books, Mummy had taught us to be readers, and at home we were expected to have a 'book on the go' at all times. Do you remember dinnertime at home with Mummy and Dad, with the four of us reading? And if we spoke there would be the withering comment 'Valerie, have you absolutely nothing to read?' And then we came to the book desert of Loreto Abbey. Perhaps the nuns felt that they occupied every moment of our time and the few spare moments should be spent on 'holy books.' But the latter were so abysmally written and a bit repetitive when you think of it. These were the years when we should have been reading the Canon (the European classics). Instead we had to do all our literary catching up in the holidays and first year at university.

You mentioned in a letter your stand-off with Mother Consiglio (Consi). I think she came to the Abbey when I was in Grade Three. She was quite a strict disciplinarian with little sense of humor, but she did cut me some slack. For Christmas I received 'Twenty-thousand Leagues Under the Sea' as a present, and brought it back to school with me to read surreptitiously at night. When you think about it, this was so daft, as the writing was excellent, the story wonderful, and there was zero sex in the book. But it was not one of the approved books on the shelves at the Abbey. I was reading it at night under the covers by torch light when Consi caught me out. She checked the book, gave it back, told me to go to sleep and not to be 'caught doing that again.' Needless to say, I continued the book by torchlight on other nights, but made sure I listened for the sound of a nun on the prowl.

ABBEY GIRLS

Dear Val,

After you left for university, you used to bring me books. Actually, you were great to visit me so often. It must have been strange to take the bus from town out to Rathfarnham, not carrying a hockey stick, and free to go into any shop you liked, chew gum, and even eat ice cream on the street! Do you remember that you brought me banned books? In 1965 in Ireland, most of the books we wanted to read were banned. I don't know where you got a hold of them, but you brought 'Lady Chatterly's Lover' and Henry Miller's 'Nexus,' or was it 'Sexus'? I didn't understand most of it, but was thrilled to be illicit. Daddy's friend Aidan Connolly brought me Nabokov's 'Lolita,' and again, I didn't quite get it but was delighted to be treated as an adult. There was one book in the School library that I remember, 'The Winds of Fortune' by Jeffrey Farnol. It was in that case of books behind the desks at the back of Grade Six Study. Hardbound, old and musty, it must have escaped detection, for it was a bodice-ripper of sorts. In contemporary terms it was incredibly tame — a tale of a young woman caught up in a swashbuckling Caribbean adventure where the hero (a pirate ship's captain) was none other than a dispossessed English Lord. Unlike Johnny Depp, he was fair-haired, and called Japhet. I resolved to name my firstborn son Japhet! Thank heavens nobody has had to live with that moniker. There were no descriptions of sex, and not even of waves lapping on the shore, but it had the right vibe, at least for a teenager.

There was a nuns' library in the main house overlooking the back of the school. There I discovered poetry.

ABBEY GIRLS

In class we had a textbook anthology of poetry from which we learned vast numbers of poems by heart. But this was where you could delve deeper — whole books of Rosetti oozing religious fervor, but also Yeats and T.S. Eliot. Because I was considered a serious pupil, I was allowed go there any time I wanted without asking permission. Nobody used the room except for oral French exams for Intermediate and Leaving Cert, so I generally had it to myself. It was a lovely room, with comfortable seats and an aura of learning. I'd go there just to get away from everyone else, as besides praying in chapel, there were few occasions when you were able to be on your own. Music practice presented an opportunity for solitude. But if a squawk wasn't heard from behind that closed door during practice, the Novice or Postulant in charge would knock on the door to make sure you weren't idling.

MUSIC

Dear Val,

    Music was a big part of our lives. You were taking the viola. I never knew why, but it seemed that by the time I got to the Abbey, I was expected to follow in your footsteps. For some reason I decided to rebel. Maybe I just wanted to take a 'small' stand and be different, the only person in my class not taking a musical instrument. But it had consequences: Mother Philippa didn't love me. We used to have music theory lessons where we would learn what an arpeggio was and how scales worked. We learned about notes, both on and in-between those strange lines, and artful clef signs, all drawn carefully on the chalkboard. I remember Mother Philippa asking the class what was the next note in an arpeggio and I shot up my hand. She pointedly said that as I wasn't taking an instrument, there was no sense in asking me for the answer. What a brilliant strategy! Within a week, I had decided to take up the viola too. My reasoning? There were lots of violins, the cello was beyond me, and I was definitely too small to play the bass.

Who taught us? We would take our instrument from that huge collection outside the concert hall and go to one of the small bedrooms over the gym. Rather like a doctor's waiting room, we'd set up the music stand (I think we had mimeographed sheets), tune the viola, and wait for a nun to come in and begin the lesson. Of course there were a few who had more exotic music lessons. CH was taking the harp from Mother Attracta who, even at that stage, was well on the way to la-la land. CH would tell her tall stories as to why she didn't know the piece, and never seemed to get into any trouble.

Do you remember music practice each evening? Some poor unfortunate Postulant or Novice had to supervise us and listen to that cacophony coming forth from each of the bedrooms for hours. We began Study at 5:00 and went to chapel at 7:00 so that meant that they had two hours, four half-hour periods, with girls ranging in ability from ghastly to reasonable. Nobody was really worth listening to. No wonder the Novices knitted or knotted those croises so ruthlessly. Actually, I don't think they let Postulants near our music practice — they would have departed the convent even before their dyed hair had grown out. But we did get Novices. And if they heard a silence emanating from one of the rooms, their job was to walk in and see why we weren't hard at work, sawing through scales furiously. What did they think we were doing instead? Well, maybe eating. I heard once that someone was getting a piano lesson in *the room where one of the girls practiced. Apparently the piano wasn't sounding right, so they opened up the top and looked in, and there they found a term's supply of Tayto crisps!*

Walking down those corridors all I ever remember is hearing strings. Still, I know some girls learned to play piano, and all the bedrooms had a piano. But an orchestra needs strings, and Mother Philippa had an uncanny ability to recruit scads of us to her service. In the orchestra there were six violas, at least six first violins and eight second violins, and then there were six cellos and three double bass. Of course you also had to have a group of youngsters waiting in the wings for the older ones to move on, rather like heifers in a dairy herd.

We had music exams too. These were fraught with stress because the examiner came 'from the State.' In other words, they weren't one of our nuns. We would be asked to play a couple of scales, a set piece that we had practiced diligently, do some sight reading, decipher a chord (my favorite), and then answer a question or two on music theory. There were eight exam grades, and I think I passed five. Mind you, I don't think anyone every failed one of those music exams.

Orchestra was exciting. Orchestra practice was on Sunday morning after Mass and breakfast, before the main meal of the day, and before visitors arrived. They had to fill the hours with something, I suppose. What else did we do on Sunday morning? Pray?

*Orchestra in the Concert Hall.
Mary is leading the viola section.*

ABBEY GIRLS

We would have got up around 7:00, gone to chapel for prayers, eaten breakfast, gone outside to run around for a while, gone to proper Mass (with singing...yeah). That would have taken us up to about 10:45, with time to rosin our bows, and get to orchestra practice. What did the girls who weren't in the orchestra do? I almost forgot — there was choir practice and lecture on Sunday morning too, and we wrote letters home on Sunday!

When I think of orchestra, I think of CS bravely manning the drums and counting furiously. She had a beatific look on her face, but she was probably just saying 'two hundred and thirty nine, two hundred and forty, two hundred and forty one,' and praying that she would still be awake by bar three hundred and ten when she was entitled to make one loud noise, and go back to her counting for another aeon. And when she missed, there would be an imperious voice from the conductor's stand calling out 'tympani — where are you?' Then there was EC, a true maestro on the organ, which had to provide all the instruments we didn't have. Watching her in action was better than a troop of whirling dervishes. Her long blond hair would be flying round her head, her hands leaping across the keys and stops, her legs furiously banging on invisible pedals. When I got to the lead chair in the violas, I was in a perfect position to see the details of her performance. EC bit her fingernails to the quick, and beyond. So a chance bang of her hand against an errant key or stop would mean that little splots of blood would shower the keys, as she heroically tried to staunch the flow, wipe up the mess, and all the while continue playing the Unfinished Symphony, with Mother Philippa putting the fear of God into her and the rest of us.

Who got to play in the orchestra? As I look at photos, there are only forty or so girls, which means that lots didn't qualify. Were they the ones who played piano instead of an instrument, or were some instrument players so bad that they were excluded? That seems hard to imagine. Pip would lead orchestra practice with us most of the time. But approaching a concert date, Miss O'Connor would come to conduct, wearing more lipstick than we had seen in years although not necessarily expertly applied. And we did speculate as to whether she wore a wig. How did she manage to bring order to our chaos? And as for the concerts — who came? I don't remember Mummy ever coming. But I remember turning pages for KH at a concert when she played a harp solo, and being very proud of my expertise at recognizing the notes on the page and knowing the optimal moment to act.

Choir; do you remember Pip separating the first and second sopranos from the altos and bass early in the autumn term? You got to stand beside someone different during choir practice — someone not in your class or even your School. Pip would man the piano and try to get us into shape — again for a concert at the end of the year. And it would have taken the whole year. I still remember learning the Halleluleh Chorus, and when I listen to it now, I recognize all the parts, and Pip's efforts to get us first sopranos to 'climb above and descend' to the highest note in the 'He Shall Reign' part.

We didn't play any musical instrument when we first came to the Abbey. We must have seemed so uneducated — though we could speak rudimentary French (thanks to Madame Tolstoy in Collon) and dance (thanks to Auntie Frank Matthews), not at all bad for culchies. How did Pip persuade you to play viola?

Dear Mary,

Don't you think everyone in Ireland was brought up playing the piano except us? I was so proud of Mummy when I was young because she forced neither Irish dancing nor piano lessons on us, because she hated both when she had to suffer through them as a child. But honestly, I think we were unique. We had no piano at home, and as long as we read and got good marks for Arithmetic and English, Mummy knew we would be well adjusted, cultured females.

Definitely, the Abbey was a shock, music-wise, as was that class in Music Theory. Everyone except me knew where middle C was! But once I got the hang of everything in music being to base eight, it was just another mathematical puzzle with different notations. And musical language was glorious — all those semi-quavers, clefs, staves, it was a secret language that opened a different world. Perhaps that explained the viola. I had a juvenile handicap with respect to the piano: my hands were thought to be way too large for the violin. But there were all of those violas that needed pupils. I think that if you wanted to continue piano the nuns approved. There were all kinds of music exams for piano, you could progress if you wanted, and definitely the piano you practiced on became 'your piano' for your time at the Abbey, and so could house all kinds of goodies, including the Taytos.

It was us, the piano uneducated and middle C limited, who got to play an instrument. Did we audition for instruments? I know that I fancied the cello, but it was already taken. If I knew what a double bass was I would have gone for that — they didn't play too often, just had to count the beat a lot, and the pitch was so low that it didn't seem possible that they could ever be out of tune. The viola was a compromise on my part I think, and by the nuns too; they knew I could beat time, but that I might not be in tune. I can't have been too bad as I found certificates for First Honours in Viola from the Royal Irish Academy of Music for two years running. I think the total musical dolts got to 'play' the triangle. That job was painful, a bit like writing 'I was late for class' a thousand times. When you think of it, they stood there for the entire practice and just had to clink at the last crescendo. But they had to be in time, have counted the beat and turned pages of music, so by the time we got to the final crescendo they must have been half dead on their feet. I loved orchestra, the pomp of it, the first violin getting to shake hands with whomever was conducting us on a formal occasion, the lag time that we had as violas (violins had more notes), and the time we had to just sit and think, and watch the sun streaming in through the long windows in the concert hall. But of course the ultimate instrument was the organ — that beautiful, powerful machine.

If nothing else we had rhythm and could beat time. Do you remember Dad balancing us on his toes and dancing around the kitchen with us to Big Band music — Tommy Dorsey type music — we had rhythm in us from our tootsies up. I think that is why we got to lead sections in the choir. Pip had me 'leading' the second sopranos at one stage, which I know was retribution on someone else, because I have a dreadful voice. But, I got the beat, and the second sopranos came in on time, even though the lead was out of tune.

I love the idea of you resisting learning to play an instrument. Good on you, but I think the nuns had a good century of training objectors and dealing with their resistance, and so they knew how to manipulate you. Now there's a solution for world problems — just use the Loreto approach: subtle manipulation. And of course the nuns could build on the borrowed Jesuit tradition, and they had dealt with the Inquisition and the counter-Reformation. So, you thought you could hold out when even Galileo gave in?

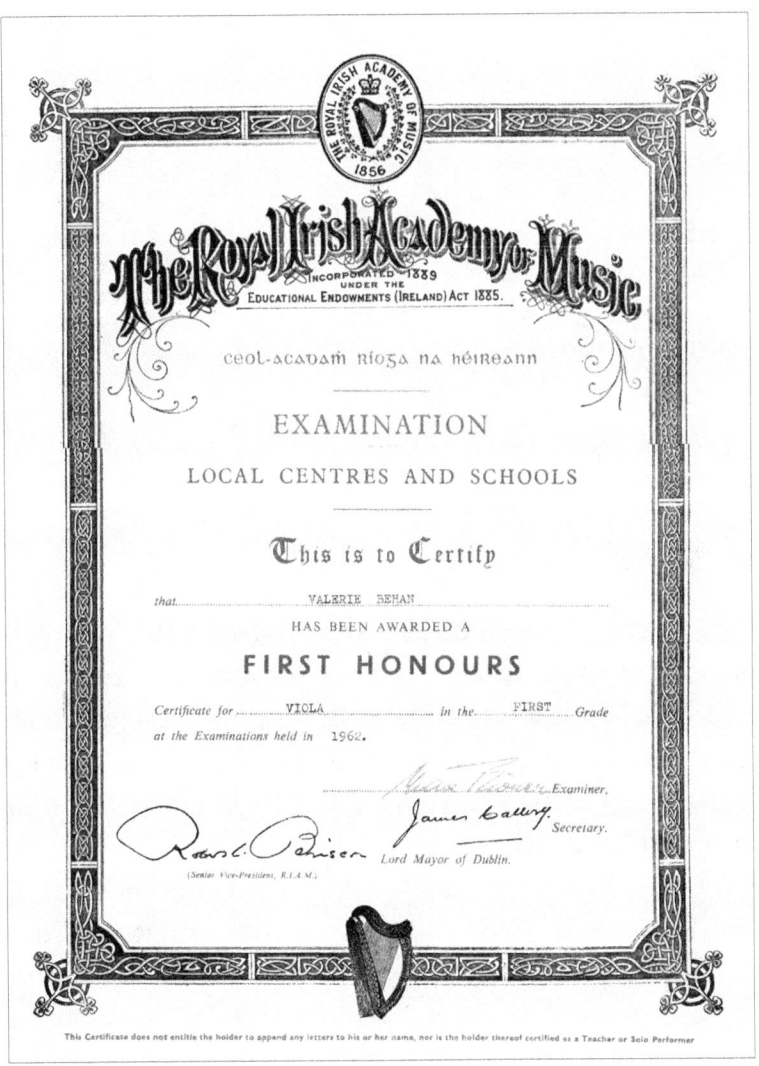

Valerie's music exam certificate for viola.

The Gym

Dear Mary,

 Your letter reminded me of the gym — it was a wonderful space, though did we do any gym-like activities there? I remember choir practice in the bleachers. And I remember dancing, especially to Strauss waltzes, the marvelous flow and rhythm of dancing, especially with someone like LT who was as tall as I was. We were in the gym, possibly practicing the foxtrot, the day in November 1963 when JFK died. I remember the nuns wheeling in the black and white TV (now where did that come from?) and all of us sobbing. Kennedy was one of ours, as close to us as a relative; we were all in shock, really devastated.

 And the gym was special because we had plays there. I know that I had no talent for acting — Mummy had told me about my lack of aplomb during some play at

St. Philomena's, which had her weeping with suppressed laughter. Mid-play I said: 'Oh. I forgot my lines,' with hand to mouth! As a result, I was never more than part of the chorus in later productions. You on the other hand had talent and I think you had speaking parts in a number of them. I know they were 'large cast' plays where most parents could expect to see their offspring dance, sing or talk. I know we did 'Charlie's Aunt,' and something with 'marbled halls' to accommodate MK's wonderful voice. Ah yes, 'The Bohemian Girl'…'with vassals and serfs by my side.'

I did get on the debating team though and I think AC, AB and LR and I got a cup for debating. It is the only photo I have of the four of us, and certainly LR would not have been on a winning sports team. I loved debating: getting a topic, arguing it from one point of view, getting passionate and committed to that stance. Some Loreto past pupils, then at University, came to debate the four of us once for practice on the topic 'Behind every great man is a woman' (they were against) and they clobbered all our arguments. Now that was a wake-up call for the narrowness of our world-view. We had Extemporary speaking also — terrifying at the outset, but a real gift don't you think?

Dear Val,

Like you, I was on the debating team. Who tutored us? Mother Emmanuel who had us for English, or Mrs. Hogan who also taught English, or was it someone else?

Each of the Loreto schools in the Dublin area competed in debate. Valerie was on the team that won in Grade Five.

Whoever it was, they were good. We went to other Loreto Schools to debate, and I loved the feeling of being an adult. In Grades Five and Six we were allowed to read the daily newspaper, laid out on a round table in a room at the end of that corridor of classrooms above the cloakroom. Did they get the Irish Times or the Irish Independent? The relevance of that wouldn't have struck me at the time, but now of course I wonder at the politics of the school and the nuns. Sadly, the team I never managed to get on was the Irish debating team. I was never good at Irish, despite twelve years of study. That debating team got to travel to boys' schools, and on one occasion we had a team of boys come to the Abbey. It was such a big event — everyone had their tongues hanging out at the presence of boys in the school that evening. Needless to say, we all attended the debate, paying close attention to whether the boys were cute, or whether they were looking in our direction. I don't remember which side won, but a few chosen girls, me included, were allowed to take tea with the boys afterwards. Years later I met one of the team — TS! He told me that the lads, who came from a day school in Clondalkin, were just as awed and curious as we were, as they had never been inside a girls boarding school before.

Plays were great fun. Obviously I was never going to be chosen for 'The Bohemian Girl' not being able to hold a note. But buried in the middle of the first sopranos for the Hallelujah Chorus, nobody would ever notice my dreadful voice. I still have vivid memories of Mother Philippa rehearsing that with us. We liked it — it was like a good musical number where everyone felt they had a necessary role. But back to plays. 'Charlie's Aunt' was a big hit.

A performance of "The Bohemian Girl." Mary (front row, third from the left) was a dancer. Valerie (back row, left) was a debonair gentleman.

The performance of "Charley's Aunt" was a great success. Mary is seated at the aunt's feet on the left.

I had a part: the daughter or the ward, I think. The nuns painted scenery, hired costumes, and put grease paint on us for the performance. Grease paint — it was certainly greasy, but as it was the only make-up ever allowed, it felt so sophisticated to wear it, if only for a night. There's a phrase from 'Charlie's Aunt' that still stays with me, 'Brazil, where the nuts come from.' By the way, I have a photo of another play we did, about the life of the nun who founded the Loreto order, Mother Mary Theresa Ball. It's a 'Suffer Little Children to come unto me' kind of tableau, and I am a fawning child over on the left, amongst many of my classmates. You are in the picture too, dressed as a nun, with your hands folded in that perfect, resigned nun way! I think you told me that CT, also playing a nun, had to have her breasts bound in a scarf because they were too prominent! LR is there too as a nun — I'd love to know what was going through her mind during the photo shoot.

We had recreation in the gym each evening, two classes together, so fifty of us in there at a time. We had a gramophone and could dance to approved records. We were allowed The Monkees, and towards the end of my time at the Abbey, a couple of Rolling Stone 45s. We had dance lessons, so knew how to waltz and foxtrot. I suppose we did the Twist, or was it banned for a few years? This was the only scheduled opportunity to fraternize with an upper or lower class, something that was definitely not encouraged by the nuns. In hindsight they must have worried about lesbianism, but as many of them were pretty ignorant of sexuality, I'm not sure.

A Loreto pageant celebrating schools in Ireland, Africa and India. Valerie (right) is dressed as a nun. Mary (front row, second from the left) is a happy schoolgirl.

At the side of the gym was a room used for Domestic Science. We had to choose Domestic Science as a subject, over Latin or Botany or German, or Physics & Chemistry — some combination of those. Needless to say, Mummy wasn't going to have us learn how to cook at the expense of Knowledge. But I envied the girls who took Domestic because they got to cook really nice things and eat them. They'd come to the refectory looking full and floury, and tell us what they had made. It looked like it was a lot more fun that Mother Carmela describing sublimation, or having us draw the vein patterns of leaves. In the end though, Mummy was right — we learned to cook on our own, and the other subjects were a lot more valuable.

Clothes

Dear Val,

    I got a present of something called 'Woolies' for Christmas this year and couldn't help remembering Mother Aloysius. She used to haunt us in winter, towering over us (she was very tall), plucking at our blouse sleeves, and asking whether we had our winter woolies on. She must have felt the cold. Well, they're back: expensive wooly t-shirts that I wouldn't have been seen dead in then, but now appreciate greatly in a Wisconsin winter. The colors have improved, and they don't pill the way our wooly vests used to. We were always cold in the Abbey in winter. I can remember lines of us huddling against the lukewarm pipes that passed through some of the classrooms. We'd clutch those pipes, despite dire warnings from the nuns that we'd get chillblains. Some of us did.

Mary's class in Grade Six. Mary is on the left in the front row, together with the Head Girl and Prefects.

Mother Carmela always wore wooly gloves with open fingers, a concession to her advanced age I suppose. The rest of the nuns were glove-less, and Mother Philippa positively radiated warmth, even if she was refereeing a match on a frozen hockey pitch. We got a drink of hot MiWadi orange juice in the evening before going to bed, and hugged those big, heavy mugs to warm our fingers before heading to cold water jugs and night-time face washing and tooth-brushing in the dormitories. The tap water was never hot enough to use a hot water bottle. But many of us had them just in case you got a cold and could persuade Sister Mercy to fill it from a kettle before going to bed early — another great winter treat.

Speaking of clothing and uniforms, do you remember the new winter coats we got one year? There was a mandate to buy them from Clerys: big, beige, belted, heavy camel-hair, which we all hated. They were the least flattering things you could imagine and nobody looked good in them. It was one thing to wear them around the grounds where they would at least keep you warm and dry, but we had to wear them to away matches, parading through the streets of Dublin where the tiny chance of a boy noticing you was completely crushed — unless he had a thing for hockey boots dangling at the end of a hockey stick. The mortification of it all.

At eleven you didn't notice the uniform, but by thirteen with breasts emerging, it was a challenge to look good. Do you remember there was a trend one year for wearing oversized cardigans? My old one had so many holes in the elbows that it could no longer be darned (we were very good at darning). Well — maybe I helped the holes along a bit. But in any case, I got money from Mummy when she next visited to buy a new one in Mother Attracta's emporium. Mother Attracta was blind enough that she didn't argue when I bought a large size. I felt so cool that year in my baggy blue cardigan, despite not yet being allowed to wear nylons. Mummy wouldn't let me wear anything but knee socks, and I wanted to be grown up like the other thirteen year-olds in my class who had breasts and thighs! I had neither, but was sure that a suspender belt would change everything. Eventually I had enough pocket money left one term (I must have saved on sweets) to buy a suspender belt from Mother Attracta, and a pair of nylons. I felt like a real woman! Of course they only lasted a few days until I got a ladder, but I darned that too.

Another trend that emerged was for crocheting Tam o' Shanters. Sewing, knitting and crocheting were all totally acceptable activities in recreation. For some reason, Tams took off in our class. Everyone learned how to make them (perhaps they were an evolution of 'useful' items like crocheted table mats), and we gave them as gifts to one another. But of course we could never wear them in school or to away matches. For that we had a blue beret. Whose idea was it that girls' schools throughout Ireland would have French berets as a necessary part of their uniform?

Divided skirts were the other item of clothing that allowed for some 'style.' We used to take them up, all the better to run on the hockey pitch, but also to show a bit of leg. They were meant to touch the ground when kneeling, but you could always argue that you had grown that term, and that your mother would let it down when you went home at the holidays. But secretly you would have turned the hem up yourself. Pressing out the telltale crease was harder to deal with. But some classmate in Domestic Science might help out with an iron; otherwise you could stash it under the mattress and sleep on it. Some of our clothing ruses remind me of the stories that Daddy used to read to us about British prisoners of war in WWII trying to escape Stalag Luft III by pretending to be appropriately clad German officers! We all agreed that the best look was a short divided skirt, the blue blazer (with the Loreto crest of course), and a beret. It didn't quite turn heads, but at least you didn't feel like a total idiot out on the streets of Dublin.

The Infirmary

Dear Val,

Did we ever get sick? I don't remember spending time in the infirmary, but I always wanted to. The best I managed was a couple of early-to-bed evenings. You'd be snuffling and blowing your nose vigorously into a hankie during class, or worse, during the quiet of evening prayers. Eventually a senior nun would relent and tell you to 'go see Sister Maxentia.' Maxie's pantry was in 'the Valley' just outside the refectory. She always seemed to be there, so I'm not sure if she had other responsibilities. She had an air of authority so I suppose she was a nurse before she became a nun. Regardless of what was ailing you, she dispensed a hot drink and two Disprin tablets. The wait-and-see approach probably worked for 99% of the ailments she dealt with, and for anything else, the doctor would be called. The prospect of a strange doctor was fairly intimidating, as all of us would have been accustomed to a family doctor who knew us inside out, and likely was present at our birth. Unlike home, you didn't think you could fool the school doctor.

If you were sent to bed early, Maxie would fill a hot water bottle out of her permanently boiling kettle. I can still remember the smell of the gas burner in her tiny kitchen, and the layer of steam fogging up the window. She'd give you hot milk or orange juice, and you could scuttle off to your dormitory and snuggle into bed, avoiding Study, chapel, music practice and recreation. Eventually, for you were rarely asleep, the noise of feet on the stairs signaled that everyone else was coming to bed, and that your brief escape from routine was at an end. You were expected to be healthy in the morning, although you might also have succeeded in getting a pass from attending Mass. That was a singular achievement.

Fainting was a great way to get sent to the infirmary. There was an urban legend that if you put wet blotting paper into your shoes, you would faint. I tried it once, but it didn't work for me. When someone did get sent to the infirmary, you knew they were really ill. There was a spate of appendicitis one year, almost an epidemic. As a result everything 'foreign' in our diet was banned: peanut butter, HP sauce, Heinz salad dressing, tomato ketchup — everything that made the food slightly more palatable. Looking back, I suppose it was an outbreak of Salmonella, but at the time there were no Carnival Cruises, so we didn't know anything about the diseases of people in confined quarters. There was a frisson of excitement as, one by one, chairs were vacated in the refectory. And when the victims eventually returned from hospital, curiosity was satisfied as they proudly showed off their surgical scars.

Sometimes girls left never to return. I don't remember anyone being expelled from our class, but someone did try to run away from school. It sounded so romantic. However, when they were eventually located, their parents were called and they disappeared. I can imagine the 'Mother Superior' tone of voice that would have been used. Parents might have had to come from the far ends of the country. Meanwhile, the 'bad' girl was confined to her dormitory or room, with a nun on guard to make sure she didn't pollute the rest of us. These departures were spoken of in hushed tones by girls and nuns alike. We were afraid to ask a direct question: what did she do? We wouldn't have got an answer in any case.

Dear Mary,

Yes we were disgustingly healthy, because I think we would have done anything for that hot water bottle in bed. In Grade One, one of my classmates, TM, ended up in the infirmary for two weeks. She had one of the catchable childhood diseases, I think mumps. I had already been through mumps (and just about everything else; Drogheda must have been a hotbed of childhood diseases) and so was allowed to visit her in the second week. I still have that feeling of envy that I had at twelve. She was in that bright infirmary sitting up in a cot that seemed so much wider than our beds in the St. Teresa's dorm, and was being coddled by Maxie with soft-boiled eggs and slivers of toast with the crusts cut off.

No one was expelled from our class either. I think we all expected someone to be expelled, at least based on all the comics and Enid Blyton stories we had read, but the nuns had quite a bit of flexibility. They must have understood the teenage angst and hormonal fluctuations that some of us were going through even though they tried to keep us occupied every waking moment. One of girls in my class had religious doubts, and I think that was a tough one for the nuns, because a few of them must have had similar doubts. For a period of time she 'lost her faith'; now they couldn't expel her for that, but she was a time bomb in a religious establishment. She was asked not to talk to any of us about what was happening to her, and to continue giving the appearance as though she still believed. In later years she described how tough it was, as she could not talk to friends about her conviction. Of course we had no guidance counselors, and somehow she had to avoid what she felt were religious transgressions, i.e., taking communion and going to confession without faith. I doubt whether the nuns would have been understanding. I think of how alone she must have felt; it's akin to realizing you are gay in today's world and being unable to share. Possibly there were other girls who shared her loss of faith, but who were better at dissembling.

Holidays

Dear Mary,

   Well it has been one of those weeks, entertaining visitors, that made me realize how different we are because we are Abbey Girls. We had that vivid disjunction between school and home life. You remember our wonderful summer trips with Mummy and Dad to the back of beyond in Spain, France Portugal, Czechoslovakia (then) and Yugoslavia (then). Dad's three weeks of holidays each summer were sacrosanct, but when you went to boarding school, he and Mummy included us in their jaunts. We would pack and pile into whatever car Dad had at the time, and the only part planned was how to get to mainland Europe. It's so easy now, but in the early 1960s it often involved the ferry from Ireland to Holyhead and then the scarper across England to get another ferry to France. Did we even stop for a meal in England? We have the photos to remind us of standing in front of Cathedrals throughout France, usually with no one else in the picture — a time when the global population was 1 billion, and there were few tourists! We stayed in such an array of places and accommodation. Do you remember the parador in Spain, the cabin near Split, the immense spa in Karlovy Vary, tiny B&B's near Lourdes, the auberge in Germany where we slept above the cows, our first experience with glorious duvets, the hotel in France down the road from a pulp and paper factory where we almost gagged from the smell? Do you remember arriving in towns in the middle of the afternoon and wandering off with Mummy, while Dad chose the accommodation, usually on the basis of what was on the evening menu?

And yet we never talked about those trips when we went back to boarding school. I don't remember writing an essay on what I did during the summer holidays. Did anyone even ask what we did in the holidays? It was as though school was one planet and home was another, and experiences were segregated, as though our teenage years alternated between parallel universes. Of course we could not have been alone in having wonderful experiences, but I know that I never asked school-friends — did you? Also, no one from school ever came home with me during holiday times or visited me during holidays. I suppose going home for the holidays was like going on one of my field trips to the Yukon, a remote, un-sharable experience. Home friends were distinct from those at school. We had sleepovers at O'Kanes in Bettystown, and with various cousins, our friends from childhood, but never with the girls we sat beside in Study or played with on hockey teams — bizarre when you think of it.

Dear Val,

Our summer holidays 'on the Continent' (it sounded so grand) could be the subject of a whole book. Like you, I remember the excitement in planning, and especially packing up the car. It always seemed to be a Ford Cortina into which Dad would have fitted extra straps and nets to store maps, a folding table and chairs, whatever. You and I would clean it within an inch of its life before the trip, for pocket money of course. All of our pocket money had to be earned. For one of the earliest trips, as there was no car ferry to England, the car was driven onto a big cargo net and slung into the hold of a cattle boat with a crane. Later, Aer Lingus began to offer a car ferry from Dublin to Cherbourg via St. Helier in the Channel Islands. The plane could carry five cars, and about twenty-five people. There's a wonderful photo of us posing in front of the plane with our car facing out from the hold beneath the cockpit. Every other year we seemed to head to Spain and Portugal, or to Germany and Yugoslavia. These weren't the traditional 'improve your mind' trips. We didn't tour museums or cathedrals; rather, we saw them fleetingly and drove on, every night fetching up in a new town. Mummy lived in fear of us not finding a room for the night, but Dad thrived on the uncertainty, believing that someone would always take us in.

There wasn't a lot to buy as souvenirs in Yugoslavia or Czechoslovakia. Spain and Portugal on the other hand *were filled with 'treasures.' Do you remember we used to buy holy pictures? It was a thing at the Abbey to send a holy picture to your best friend with 'In rems of...' written on the back to commemorate some event that you had shared. The only holy pictures available in Ireland at the time were the typical religious saints and martyrs, Christ on the Cross, and Mary looking virginal. In Spain we found El Greco Christs, and cartoon-like Mary's that we carefully doled out during the next school year amongst our friends.*

It was only after a few years of these holidays that I realized how much fun Dad got in smuggling stuff back to Ireland. He used to take the air filter out of its compartment above the carburetor and hide a stash of stainless steel cutlery, something that was commonplace in Germany, but unavailable in Ireland. Another favorite hiding place was the spare wheel well, although he also stashed things in the wheel hubcaps until they made too much of a racket. Mummy was always suspicious when he would tell both us to go off walking with her, as we usually split up in the evenings for our pre-dinner walk. That's when he bought cheap Spanish brandy and put it into plastic bladders concealed behind the door panels of the car. It wasn't as if he liked it, or even drank it when we got home. Nor could Mummy serve it to guests with any confidence, as he would have transferred it to old whiskey bottles with mismatched corks. He just loved the thrill of it all.

You are right; we never shared these stories with our school friends. They wouldn't have understood. Nobody went abroad in those days. The standard summer holiday for everyone we knew was a rented house by the sea. Mind you, I was envious of that sort of holiday. You could talk about it and all your friends would understand what it was like, and how much fun it was. But I wouldn't trade, not then and not now. We were incredibly fortunate to have been introduced to foreign travel so early in our lives — the pure, uninhibited joy of it all.

The Abbey waiting our return after the holidays.

WHAT IS MEMORY?

Dear Val,

This is my last letter to you about the Abbey. I remember the first one I wrote so vividly. It was the one about getting letters delivered to us in the refectory at dinner. I wrote it almost exactly two years ago, and that was the beginning of this wonderful, sisterly journey. I'm going to miss our letters very much.

Being a neuroscientist, I cannot help thinking about the 'how' and 'where' of these memories. Writing that first letter to you, I could put myself in the refectory with the clamor of talk and banging of dishes and the scraping of chairs all around. I could see the details: the color of the walls, the location of the windows and doors, the height of the ceiling. And as I wrote, I went further and further into those details, layering onto the scene where each class sat, how many girls were at each table, what the chairs looked like, the shape of the teapots. Oddly enough, even now I cannot 'see' the design of the cups or plates, although I do remember the shape of serving platters. Where in my brain is this all stored? And how? Why are some features easy to recall and others not?

Your first letter in reply to mine let me see what you were seeing, as it were. I had expected that our memories would be more or less identical. Your description of our pre-Abbey days is exactly as I remember my first eleven years in Drogheda. So I was taken aback to see that you had completely different ways of looking at the whole boarding school scene, despite our overlapping there by four years. Where I saw order, you saw chaos. Where I was thinking about whether I'd get a letter from a boy (when I was of an age to care), you were worrying about a response to LR's prank request for you to join the Missions as a nun! Where you were a reluctant Head Girl, I was lusting after that moniker. It struck me then that despite our overwhelming similarities, we saw our Loreto world through completely different eyes. At this age (in our 60s), most people who know both of us well would agree that we are remarkably similar. It's not too surprising that we are biologically alike. The fact that you have a corn that flares up occasionally between the exact same toes as mine, or that we get patches of dry skin in the same places in winter, reminds me that there's a striking overlap in our genetic makeup. Even more surprising was when I told you about I dream that I had the other night: that I was driving a double decker bus, but the steering wheel was located on the upper deck at the front, making it really hard to steer around traffic and people. To my amazement you said that you have that dream too. How can that be? Surely not everyone born in Ireland dreams of out-of-control double decker buses?

Mummy and Daddy did their level best to treat us identically while we were growing up. We were even dressed alike for the first few years. As there were only two of us, wherever you went, so did I until you went to the Abbey. We even shared a bedroom at home. So, epigenetically I would expect there to be a big overlap as well. The first time we were really apart was when you went to boarding school. For the next two years I followed your every move. I looked forward to going to the Abbey to visit you every second Sunday with Mummy, and hung on everything you said about the place. We were together again at the Abbey for the next four years, and even shared a bedroom one year. So how is it that we see some things so differently, yet many of our letters describe surprisingly similar memories? It's as if we're viewing the same 3-D image, but with the perspective shifted slightly. The shift might be only ten or twenty degrees, but looking at it from a forty-five year distance, it has grown much larger.

Despite the differences in our memories of the Abbey, your letters opened doors into areas of my brain that I had no clue were still there. That was such a pleasure — to get a letter from you and be taken by the hand into my past! It was as if I were there in real time. All of my senses were awoken. I could wander around the school in my mind, hear the sound of music practice, remember the smell of boiled mutton and the taste of canned peas, feel the warmth of the heating pipes and the cool of a drizzle during morning *rounds. There were layers upon layers of memories just waiting for me to explore them. It has been an incredible feast, and I'm sad to see the end of it.*

I know enough about the brain to understand that memories are basically synaptic connections between neurons. While I am reading one of your letters, an action potential is triggered in a nerve cell and travels along its axon to a synapse at the end. There, a packet of neurotransmitter is released into the gap between the nerve cell and adjacent ones, and ideally starts more action potentials in these nerve cells, and on ad infinitum. But your letters triggered a myriad of memories that I didn't know I had in me. I cannot imagine that these nerve cells have been lying low for the past 45 years, just waiting for the chance to spring into action, or that packets of neurotransmitter in synapses all over my brain are holding their breath, as it were, on the off chance that they will be called upon to function today. But they do. It's easier for me to imagine a network of nerve cells with millions of connections, always at the ready. Reading your letter starts a trigger at a certain, unique place in this network, resulting in a cascade of memories for me. Each one of those memories can trigger even more permutations and combinations of activity in the network, and so my memories of the Abbey grow and become alive.

But if that's the case, why are certain memories closed to me? For example, I cannot 'see' you in the Abbey. I can reason that you were there, that you sat in the same room as me for every meal for four years, that you slept in the bed next to me for a year, that you played in the same section of the orchestra for three years, prayed in the same chapel and sang in the same choir. Yet, try as I might, I cannot conjure an image of you, other than taking one from my mental iPhoto library.

Do you remember the last time we went back? It was 2007 or thereabouts. The two of us had been driving around Dublin looking at old haunts, and somehow found ourselves taking that well-worn path through Rathmines towards Rathfarnham. We passed the Sisters of Charity convent at Harold's Cross, crossed the Dodder River, headed uphill past Rathfarnham Castle, drove through Rathfarnham Village, turned the corner at the Yellow House pub, and there it was. It still took my breath away in all of its grey, granite splendor. That was the view that was either dreaded (by you) or desired (by me) for six years.

The gates were open, so we drove in that sweeping driveway up to the main house. But the grass was uncut and there were weeds in the gravel. We parked the car and looked up towards St. Joseph's dormitory where we had shared a room one year. The litany of 'do you remembers' started, and we spent half an hour or so exchanging memories and stories. It was both wonderful and sad. We knew that the Abbey had closed, but I don't think we were prepared for the neglect. It seemed like a place that would last forever.

In May 1999, I flew home from the USA for the final Abbey Reunion. The past pupils association must have gone into high gear to find and contact every single Abbey girl around the globe who was still alive. TC from Termonfeckin found my e-mail address and contacted me about it. Without further ado, I bought a ticket and came home to Ireland for four days. I was in the midst of teaching and final exams were approaching, but I didn't care. Somehow I knew this would be an important day that I did not want to miss.

The evening before the reunion, our class met at a pub in Donnybrook where I've not been in 30 years at least. I remember walking in behind JM and looking around at this huge group of women, and scanning them to see if anyone looked familiar. They honestly didn't! Then I saw BC, and I began to smile, and then to laugh and laugh and laugh. Gradually other faces took shape and tugged at my memory. If I wasn't smiling openly all night, I certainly was inside. I kept sneaking looks at people to try to fix their 'new' faces in my mind, looking at their clothes (no uniforms!), watching their expressions. The challenge of talking to people you have not seen in more than thirty years is overwhelming. Where do you begin? What's important? Husbands? Careers? Children? Strangely, what struck me about the whole reunion was that there was far less interest in the intervening years, or who or what one had become or done, but rather, a maelstrom of memories that needed to be announced or confirmed. For example, BC told me that I had once loaned her my new hockey stick, for she had broken hers and was due to play an important match. My first thought was why had I done that? What was my motive? But that's the older mind trying to analyze a terribly simple gesture of a fourteen-year-old girl.

I'm so sorry that you weren't there. What an amazing event! Over a thousand Abbey girls returned, ranging in age from sixteen to ninety. You'll have to take my word for it, but at least my description is fairly accurate because afterwards, when I returned to the USA, I wrote to those in my class who weren't at the reunion, trying to recapture the essence of the event and share it with them.

We rounded that last corner by the Yellow House pub (yes, it was still there), and came within sight of the Abbey. I have to admit it looked very foreboding and intimidating. We parked behind the building on the 'Seconds' hockey pitch as a huge, white marquee had been erected on the 'Firsts' pitch. Other women were arriving, older ones and younger ones, and each wore the same slightly apprehensive look, but walked to the building with shoulders straight, and with an air of mission accomplished successfully — life's mission as an Abbey girl, that is.

We went in by the door between the cloakroom and the refectory and registered. The desks were manned by endless Loreto Beaufort uniform-clad young girls. Each six-year cohort was given a similar colored nametag. My cohort (1961-67) was pink, and at odd moments you'd see a pink name, squint at it, and screech a familiar name, laughing all the while. Of course, just as you would be doing this, another encounter would be occurring between two or more other girls with different colored nametags, whom you'd never seen before, but who looked as if they owned the place, just as you did.

After a while I drifted away from JM as I really wanted to savor the experience by myself. So I walked first through the refectory where tables were set with wine glasses! It was spotless and pristine, and with the exception of there being no podium for a presiding nun, it looked exactly as I remembered it from years past. I checked the ceiling — there were no butter pats or inverted silver goblets hanging precariously from it! Next I went through the side door of the refectory to the gym. In the Valley someone was talking about Sister Maxentia's pantry and the Infirmary, and once again a flood of memories returned.

The gym seemed so small. The Domestic Science room was filled with caterers getting lunch ready for the thousand plus who would attend. The bleachers were still there, and there were ropes, something that would have been unheard of in our time! The stage looked so empty of props, and small too. But the memories were wonderful — of 'Charley's Aunt' and 'A Waltz Dream' and 'The Bohemian Girl.' By now I had a permanently affixed grin on my face that broke into a broad smile as a particularly juicy story from the past jumped into my brain. I walked up the back staircase to the Science room, but it was locked. I could see the arched windows and high benches that I remembered through a slit in the door. I wondered why they kept us out of there, for absolutely everywhere else was open. Considering this was the site of the inception of my career (although little did I know it at the time), I really wanted to imbibe the room's atmosphere. Speaking of atmosphere, there were no smells that registered, at all, anywhere. I had expected some, because smell was a big part of my memory of the Abbey. I came down the back staircase to Lisieux and St. Cecelia's dorms. The art room had been split in two to make a computer room and a teachers' common room. That was a lovely, light-filled room once, although I have memories of powdered paint and absorbent paper, and the utterly hideous compositions that I produced there for Mother Carmela.

The order of the day was for Mass (of course!) in the marquee, followed by a light lunch, and then time to wander and remember, before a closing ritual. After Mass, we were welcomed by the last of the remaining nuns from our time, Mother Fidelis and Mother Paulinus. I have to admit that Mass in a tent on the hockey pitch was a little strange. I missed the chapel and the organ, but it would have been impossible to fit us all in there. For lunch there were tables laid everywhere — the gym, the stage, the Valley, and even in the nun's refectory which we had never been privy to in the past. As luck would have it, our cohort was seated in the refectory. The class of 1967 occupied two center tables (where Grades Five and Six used to sit) and proceeded to talk, all together, and all loudly. It was a grand lunch although I didn't take note of what we ate. At one stage JD (three years my senior and a genuinely funny woman), got up to give a speech. As nobody was listening to her, and only those close by could hear (the cacophony was alarming), she got up on a chair. The shock was that there was no nun to strike her down dead, or at least demand a Merit or Deportment point!

After lunch I headed off again to explore my Memory Palace. Onward to the concert hall, still a sublime room. There were photographs all around the walls, of previous concerts, with the year marked. Next I wandered to the chapel, past the little box where Pip played organ, and the room where we had confession. I checked out the pews where we sat for Mass in the mornings and prayers each evening. How did they fit us all into those few benches, wearing our veils, and being so obedient under Mother

Fidelis' eagle eye? That's where I first read the Bible, the unabridged version, and was more than entertained.

I headed towards the Parlour and the main entrance hall. These and the various priests' parlours off it were beautifully decorated and refurbished. By now on my tour, rooms were becoming hugely full and crowded, and the babble was overwhelming. There was little time for meaningful conversations, but eavesdropping on others was so much fun. I kept going upward, to St. Teresa's dormitory, now empty of beds. The cubicles were separated by wooden partitions, not curtains as in the old days, and some of them even had proper washbasins. But the layout was essentially the same, and the sun still streamed in through the coveted windows. Then up another flight of stairs to St. Joseph's, now very shabby and neglected. But here the eavesdropping was best. Jo's made an impression on everyone who lived there. Someone mentioned watching the planes coming in to the airport from up there, someone else remembered smoking, and someone else said they used to climb out the window and sit on the roof. I think my happiest years were in St. Joseph's, especially the year I shared a bedroom with you.

Onward, to the long corridor with the big mirror at the end of it. The same pictures were still on the wall: Vermeer's head of a girl with pearl earrings, a Laughing Cavalier, some French Impressionists, and others that I recognized as being amongst the greats. Next I headed to the classrooms which seemed huge, way too large for 30 paltry desks. I listened as someone with a pink nametag told me where I sat, where she sat, and who occupied the rest of the back row. I asked: 'But who sat in front?,' and another class mate admitted that it was her unlucky fate to be under the presiding nun's eagle eye. These rooms were empty of furniture, but if you closed your eyes, it all fell into place so quickly: warming our hands on the heating pipes, Mother Carmela falling off the podium and breaking her leg, Pip asking for Latin declensions before the prayers began, wearing white sheets while acting out 'Julius Caesar' for Mother Emmanuel, study periods on Sundays, and so much more. More photographs from the past lined these walls, and now I could see Mrs. Hogan. I had forgotten her face.

I climbed the staircase to St. Anne's dormitory above the classrooms. It seemed different and I heard an elderly female voice asking: 'where are the horse boxes?' But as I rounded the corner, there they were in full splendor. Of course I looked to the corner where the nun's cubicle used to be, remembering the shadows they would cast on the ceiling after lights out as they undressed by candlelight. Their aberrant shadow forms were far more intimidating than their real presence — hollow voices calling out in the dark: 'will the girl who is out of her bed return to it immediately!'

We returned to the big white tent for a brief departure speech. Here tears flowed. It was hard not to admire those nuns, past and present. It was also impossible to ignore those hundreds of brave, strong women who truly changed other peoples' lives in quiet and subtle ways in some cases, and in big ways too. There are no Nobel laureates amongst the Abbey girls, no world leaders, but there are amazing women who know that they were exposed to a unique educational experience that changed them forever — the *majority for the better. Sure there were a few for whom the Abbey must have been a nightmare. Nonetheless, it was wonderful to look out on that sea of women and discover that the vast majority of each class who are still living, came back to see the Abbey one more time. For each one, it was a magical day.*

I don't want to go back to the Abbey ever again. I want it all to remain frozen in a time capsule in my memory. Unfortunately the process of memory doesn't really allow for that. However, writing these letters has allowed me to consolidate and enhance the way I choose to remember the Abbey, and your letters have validated most of those memories. That's enough for now and for the future.

Dear Mary,

Ah yes, what is memory? Your letters have been like a Keats' poem opening a magic casement for me. Like you, I wish I could 'see you' at the Abbey — but I don't. I see the nuns' faces, those of classmates, even those I've haven't seen since 1965, but you are a ghost. We were not 'friends' before the Abbey — we were too close in age as sisters. I being the eldest did not particularly want to share experiences with you, as it often meant that I lost and you gained! And I wasn't caring, but then you were a terrible tease — remember your tormenting me with 'Hairy Molly' caterpillars? At Loreto Abbey classes were quite segregated, we did not share space per se except orchestra and the shared room in St. Josephs when we were older. It took me a while to learn to be a kind sister.

ABBEY GIRLS

Our shared dreams are easy to interpret. The source of the one about the double decker bus must refer to going to University College Dublin in Belfield. Remember how we always got the bus from Leeson Street, which was close to Loreto Hall where we were in residence? We would rush to the top and front of the bus because that was where many friends would be. Like our trips to Belfield, those dreams are exciting, and always in technicolor, with a mixture of narrow streets, other vehicles that we really can't see from the top of the bus, narrow turns and so many people. They have an element of 'Slumdog Millionaire' about them.

But that dream lacks the prolonged worry of my Abbey dreams. I know that I have the one where I am late for Study and am not allowed in. I am running along the corridor peering in through the windows to the various Study rooms, and I can't find my fellow classmates. Worse, when I do find them, I'm ignored and effectively shut out. And yet, I don't remember anyone being ostracized at the Abbey. I think our upbringing and the nuns tried to ensure that we were inclusive and included. A nightmare that is rarer now is sitting an exam and not having studied for it, really not being prepared at all. It is always a written Irish exam and I walk into the exam hall to incomprehensible gobbledygook. Now that is strange, because I was good at written Irish. Memory is strange.

Most importantly your letters remind me of what I owe Loreto Abbey for introducing me to amazing women, both the nuns who taught us, Mrs. Hogan, and especially other pupils, who have achieved academic and other successes that leave us in the dust. You asked me why I didn't go back to that last reunion. I know that many of my classmates felt that as Head Girl of the cohort 1959-1965, I should have been there. But I don't regret not returning. My memories remain those of the Abbey when I was there as a pupil: an experience of homesickness, pleasure at my surprising success at school, pride in shared accomplishments such as the Debating Cup and Hockey Cup, and overall happiness that those days are over. We have been extraordinarily lucky in our lives and have had wonderful experiences subsequent to the Abbey, but Loreto Abbey was not a happy experience for me. I could try and dissect the 'why' of the difference in our experience, but it would all be speculative. When I remember the Abbey I think of the absence of freedom.

More important though is the reality of what the Loreto experience gave us. Our careers have brought us to out of the way locations, in my case, northern Siberia, Alaska, arctic Canada and Central America. We have been in physically and sociologically challenging situations and survived. But then, we survived the Abbey! You and I know what that means: the Abbey has taught us how to live independently, how to persevere, how to negotiate our surroundings, and how to have a positive effect wherever we are. Now, that is high accolade for any teaching establishment.

Mary and Valerie in 1967

ACKNOWLEDGMENTS

A number of friends were instrumental in helping us write this book. Many thanks go to our class-mates at Loreto Abbey Rathfarnham, especially those of the cohorts 1959-1965 and 1961-1967, who helped us negotiate the wonders and terrors of the Abbey. They added the humour, the competition, the repartee and, most of all, the friendship that made our boarding school years as exceptional as they were. They helped form the people we became. Very special thanks go to our husbands, Guy Pelletier and Tim Heggland, for their incisive inputs on this book and for their patience over the years with two opinionated Abbey Girls.

www.ingramcontent.com/pod-product-compliance
Lightning Source LLC
Chambersburg PA
CBHW072156070526
44585CB00015B/1174